Contents

Each of you carry within you your own thoughts and ideas about what it means to be psychic. Many of you see this as something separate from your everyday life, but this is not so. To be alive is to be psychic. It is time to realize your creativity and power – all of your life is a creative, psychic endeavor.

Gay Bonner

Being Alive is Being Psychic

Being
Alive
is
Being
Psychic

Sandra J. Stevens

Cordella

A Division of Station Hill Press

Published by Cordella Books, a division of Station Hill Press, Barrytown, New York 12507.

Typeset, designed, and produced at Open Studio, Ltd. Rhinebeck, New York 12572.

Library of Congress Cataloging in Publication Data
Stevens, Sandra J., 1938-
    Being alive is being psychic.

    1. Psychical research. 2. Stevens, Sandra J.,
1938-   . 3. Psychical research — Biography.
I. Title.
BF 1031.S79   1982   133.8   82-18208
ISBN 0-930794-81-8

First Edition

Manufactured in the United States of America.

Preface

SHEILA REYNOLDS AND I had been conducting our psychic business, Mind Matters, for about a year when we met Kitty West in the autumn of 1978. Kitty came from New York for a consultation with Gay Bonner, our non-physical friend who uses the medium of Sheila's body to communicate with those of us currently living in physical bodies. "Talking to Gay" constitutes the largest portion of our work with Mind Matters, although we also offer seminars, workshops, and classes on psychic development, reincarnation, and self-hypnosis as well as private hypnosis sessions.

Kitty was a literary agent. It was she who suggested this book, enthusiastically encouraging me to put my creative wheels in gear and write it. That autumn day, after listening to Gay's words for her, Kitty began asking us questions about how we started doing what we were doing, how we liked it, how it affected our lifes, and so on. Since people frequently asked us these questions, we had a "routine" – stories we each told, taking turns where appropriate. Kitty urged me to write down these stories, stressing that people who have such experiences seldom write about them while they are fresh and new. I balked. I wanted to write but not autobiography.

During the next few weeks, however, an idea kept coming into my mind. Many of the people Sheila and I were seeing were new to psychic experience. Like us, they had begun to experience paranormal happenings that were causing them to question old concepts, old teachings, conventional ways of perceiving, and, most importantly, their role in the creation of their lives. Much of what we (and, of course, Gay Bonner) were saying over and over to these people had to do with the naturalness of psychic experience and how to use personal power in the day-to-day unfolding of one's life. It seemed to me that there was a need for a "psychic how-to" book for beginners – people who wanted to fully understand and use their new experiences in a concrete, constructive manner. I checked the occult sections of the bookstores. Most of the "how-to" books available consisted of dry lists of instructions or were steeped in heavy religious dogma that insisted on a "path" or "method" involving a particular belief system. The autobiographical books on the same shelves were mostly first-person accounts of how unique and special the authors were. I found most of them boring by the end of the third chapter and was further convinced that I did not want to write a strictly first-hand account.

Another letter from Kitty arrived. She again urged me to write "just a little autobiographical piece." I groaned. Then it hit me! I could write the "how-to" book I had been thinking about but I could weave our experiences into the book as examples and anecdotes. These, I hoped, would serve as a guide to my readers while they (as we had been doing) became aware of their psychic selves and integrated their experiences, psychologically and intellectually, into their beings. I had found my direction and purpose: *Being Alive is Being Psychic* was conceived. Gestation and birth took two years.

Sheila's help, of course, has been invaluable. Although I did the actual writing, she supplied me with her notes, suggestions, accounts of her experiences, encouragement, and of course, Gay's words and wisdom. Sheila's input was my initial reason for writing this book in the third person. It is her book as well as mine, and I wanted it to be written from both our perspectives. Later, I realized that I had even a deeper motivation, and that was to "objectify" my own experiences so that, for my own psychological reasons, writing about myself would be easier. I also believed that a novelistic, third-person approach would make paranormal or psychic experience less unique and indi-vidual, and more universal. Our message is always that everyone is psychic and that such experiences are available to all who pay atten-tion to them.

Chapters 1-4 are about Sheila and me – our relationship to each other and to Gay Bonner, our unusual friend and guide. Beginning with Chapter 5, we explore different areas of psychic development, using our personal stories and those of people we have met to offer the reader specific and concrete suggestions for exploring his or her unique psychic nature. Sheila and I are very different individuals and so is our approach to various experiences. We have found, however, that our experiences have had an amazingly consistent interweaving of learning which, time and again, has forced us to admit to what can only be an orderly plan for personal growth, through which we are somehow connected, yet also free and unique. It is this loving plan that we wish to impart to the reader – a plan in which we believe everyone shares. To be alive is to be psychic, and we all have the ability to expand our awareness into our psychic and spiritual natures.

A special thanks goes, of course, to Kitty West for her encouragement and support. I also wish to give special thanks to Virginia Wurster Ramus for her lovingly critical reading of the manuscript. I also ask all my many friends (visible and invisible) who contributed their experience, their love, and their guidance, to please accept my gratitude.

Sandra J. Stevens

Chapter 1

First Experiences

ONE WARM APRIL DAY, Sandy settled into an old rocking chair in an upstairs bedroom to meditate. Her therapist had taught her to sit quietly and repeat a word which had no meaning for her. "It will relax you, center you, and give you energy when you're tired." She found this to be true and so every once in a while she would sit and feel the relaxation move over her body as she repeated "ha ring" (or something like that) over and over in her mind. On some occasions she would feel a vibration moving up from her feet throughout her body. She concluded that this was the energy her therapist had spoken about.

This particular day, Sandy was very tired and wanted a quick rest. As she sat there feeling the vibrations move up her body, she simply observed the sensation without much interest or involvement. But when the vibrations reached her head, instead of stopping and beginning again or leaving, they continued right up through the top of her head. Suddenly she realized that these vibrations – this energy – was *her,* and her consciousness was now outside of her body somewhere just above her head; and somehow it (she) was attracted to what she "knew" was another presence or being just above that. Feeling a mounting excitement, but knowing what was happening was okay, she – this energy that was now her and out of the body she had always believed was her – "touched" or "connected" with whatever it was there above her in her bedroom, on this warm sunny day, where she could also hear her children playing below and outside.

It was just a "touch," but when it was over and she had settled back in her familiar warm body, she felt a flood of joy and peace rush over her, and the world in which she had always lived changed. Nothing ever was to be the same again.

Subjectively, Sandy's experience was dramatic and exciting. High points or "peak experiences," as Abraham Maslow called them, are intense happenings that can change us, but usually only temporarily, unless we find the means to integrate them meaningfully into the patterns of our lives.

When confronted with new data, Sandy's usual response was to find a book or books to explain it to her. After the bedroom experience, she began reading related books that somehow began presenting themselves to her — another kind of "coincidence" she would soon take for granted. Until the incident in the rocking chair, Sandy's world view had been what might be described as university-produced existential agnosticism. We are here. What we know, we know because of our senses. If there was a God, he must have died as reported, or the world would not be in such a miserable state. Her life, as all life, was an accidental happening, and she never thought that there may be anything beyond the evidence given her by her five physical senses. This view, intellectual in nature, unconsciously conflicted with an innate optimism reflected in a belief that life could and would improve—both her own and the rest of the world's. As a young woman, she had worked actively for various political causes and then, after reaching her thirties and a crisis in her marriage, entered therapy and directed her energy and optimism inward.

It was in group therapy that she first met Sheila. They began attending group sessions about the same time in the fall of 1973. Sandy had attended the weekly sessions one or two times before Sheila started. Their meeting seemed inconsequential at the time but was to take on much more significance several years later.

During that first group session, Sheila talked of her then husband, describing many of her feelings and impressions about their relationship. Sandy later walked up to her and remarked that he sounded very much like her current lover. Later they found out that the two men knew each other well and had worked together for several years — a coincidence. Both women, new to the group, were very frightened by the sessions. The therapy was emotive in nature, involving much screaming and active expression of feeling. Sheila was not sure she planned to return, but during that week she dreamed of Sandy. The dream gave her confidence to return, and when she related it to the group, Sandy felt very good — she had been noticed and someone liked her — another even more important coincidence.

Three or so years went by. Sandy and Sheila would see each other occasionally — sometimes socially, or sometimes in the evershifting weekly sessions, or at an all-night marathon. Both women broke up their marriages, took new lovers, new jobs, new living situations.

The therapy worked well for them. They each became ready for the events leading to this book.

Sheila's experiences with her psychic potential did not begin with a single and definite experience as did Sandy's. She had always had feelings about the world which repeatedly told her that the way she viewed reality differed from those around her. She learned at an early age to hide the differences. As a young child, Sheila talked often to her imaginary playmates. She played and lived in a world others around her could not see. They called her "crazy," and she believed them. She harnessed her inner life with an outward show of conventional behavior. All the questions about this inner reality bounced off the walls of her consciousness and, as they did, she strove harder to keep them quiet and subdued so that she would be like other people. When she could "see" that most people's faces and words never seemed to match their feelings and thoughts, she kept quiet. Her thoughts and her knowing that life was more than boundaries of her body and the length of her physical life remained unexpressed. She had no one to talk to about her mind, her feelings, the dreams, fantasies and various states of consciousness which were her and which made her different and crazy.

As with Sandy, books became her way of finding answers. If the people around her could not understand her kind of thinking, perhaps there were others who wrote about such things. She discovered Alan Watts, who talked to her about expanded consciousness and alternate ways of "seeing." She understood him and knew that he would understand her as no one had. She felt her own thoughts and feelings mirrored back to her. She read and read. Mostly books on psychology, anything on the mind. The therapy sessions helped her begin to accept her reality as valid.

She began to experiment. In her books she read about self-hypnosis. She tried it. She had been going through a particularly difficult time in her life. She and her husband had just separated. Lying on the beach alone, she decided to try to induce a trance state. Part by part, she consciously began relaxing her body. An hour went by before she finished; but when she did, a profound sense of peace enveloped her entire being—body and mind. She knew that she had never before completely relaxed. She lay there feeling very good, when suddenly she sensed a light around her, brighter than the sunshine she experienced moments before. She "felt" a presence, a presence she "knew" to be a grandmother who had died before her birth. This was not someone she thought of consciously, and she was surprised to experience this "knowing" that it was her grandmother.

This incident spurred her on to further experimentation. Daily now, she took time to induce hypnotic trance. She did it for the sense of peace and relaxation she found, but she also continued to have subjective and paranormal experiences. She often felt in touch with her grandmother. Occasionally she felt she could delve into her own past and converse with the child she had once been. These experiences were very real to her but she still felt she had no one to share them with. They were "crazy."

Finally, she took a risk. She talked about the self-hypnosis to her boss and he gave her the name of a friend who was interested in hypnosis. She began to meet with Joe Cook and his wife, Rose. Here she could talk about some of her experiences. Joe is a hypnotist, and the three of them experimented.

Sheila had a phobia about elevators which caused her much discomfort in her daily life. She talked to Joe and Rose about this fear and they decided to see if they could discover a cause. Sheila had not encountered the source of her discomfort in her therapy sessions. Joe hypnotized her and began regressing her backward in time.

"Okay, Sheila. You are now ten years old. Do you still fear elevators?" Sheila nodded yes.

"You are now eight years old. Do you still..."

They continued this procedure until age five. There they found the fear gone. Joe slowly moved her up from five years old to five years one month, two months, three months – at five years seven months, Sheila began crying. She then related a long-forgotten memory of having been accidentally locked in the bathroom for hours before being found by her parents. Her mother later confirmed the incident. Her fear of elevators lessened with the reliving of the experience.

Many times in her therapy sessions she had experienced the power of the subconscious to release material which would make behavior changes possible. This was the first similar experience using hypnosis. Later it would become extremely important when she and Sandy would meet Dick Sutphen and decide to become past-life regressive hypnotists.

Meanwhile, Sandy read her books. Later they found they had been reading the same books – books such as Adam Smith's *Powers of Mind,* John Lilly's *Center of the Cyclone, The Secret Life of Plants,* and most importantly, Jane Roberts' Seth books. Sandy meditated on a regular basis now. That shot of pure joy was more addicting than anything she had ever encountered, and she wanted more. She did continue to have reinforcing experiences in meditation – wonderful feelings of well being; glimpses into parts of her mind that contained scenes and dramas she knew did not come from her present life experience but that she knew were real; spontaneous answers to problems jumping into her mind from seemingly nowhere. Most important, however, was the continuing change in her perception. The world looked different – its beauty springing out at her in new and exciting ways. She was beginning to develop what she would later recognize as a new consciousness – one in which she could see things as they are, in the moment, without the old clouded defenses which had always characterized her interactions with the world in the past. This new consciousness was dynamic, a growing awareness that happens still; and the stretches of time she enjoyed this awareness were expanding.

Such perception was still a long way off, however. During that summer, as she read she also experimented. She had friends who were seeking answers from Eastern metaphysical disciplines. She talked to them and found that her subjective experiences were more common than she had guessed. She began to realize how limiting her education had been – limited by a severely myopic point-of-view that stressed logic, accepting only that which could be confirmed by the senses with empirical evidence to support every supposition. She had been taught that the world came about because of a great cosmic accident which brought together elements that combined to give us what we see around us. Acceptance of that hard cold fact meant, of course, that we were totally alone, individual, and destined to be relatively shortlived – both as individuals and as a universe. Our only comfort was that we were all in it together, so a humanistic approach was the most sensible one to have. There was no God or collective unconscious, no life after death, no interconnectedness other than the "all in the same boat" feeling.

So Sandy visited an ashram and had a blissful, inexplicable experience with a traveling guru. She wondered if she would be packing herself off to India. Some of her friends already had. The idea scared her. She had to know. She had to find out more about was happening to her, but she had trouble with the rigidity of the Eastern disciplines – all the "have to's" and "musts." She had had enough rules of her own throughout her life and instinctively knew she did not need to add someone else's to those. The learning would have to be in her own way. She returned to the ashram for a second time and the confusion cleared. She then knew she was not going to India. She had also started reading Jane Roberts' *The Seth Material,* and found that what she read there better explained her feelings. She could identify with Jane Roberts' struggles with her experiences — her skepticism and caution.

In August, Sandy sailed along the New England coast on a windjammer. This was the first vacation she had taken completely alone since before her marriage. The experience of sailing was two-fold and, in a sense, framed. Everyone — some forty people of mixed demography — would gather for breakfast, then lunch, then supper, and finally, in port, for nightly activities. This part of the trip was social — a lot of fun. During the in-between periods, Sandy found a quiet spot at the front of the hundred-foot schooner where each day she would take her mat, her books, and her glasses and lie there, enjoying the to-and-fro rocking of the boat. She never read the books. The hypnotic spell of the rocking catapulted her into what she later realized were trance states — altered states of consciousness — where something important was happening to her. She would have no memory of the content of these trances, but throughout the week and for a long time afterward she had a sense of well-being, a sense that whatever happened to her during those natural trances was for her good. Trying to explain these feelings to her therapy group led her to Gay Bonner, spiritual guide.

It was a Tuesday night session — the "women's group." Most of the people had been meeting together for a couple of years. They knew one another well — or rather, they knew one another's deepest feelings and secrets but very little about the day-to-day events of their lives. Sheila had joined this group several months before. Shifting of the group members occurred frequently, and most everyone in the society that grew under her therapist's direction knew the others. Sandy was trying to talk about the things that were happening to her. She had not tried before, but now she wanted to express that feeling she had of "everything working out for the greater good." It was much more than an optimistic feeling or simply "being in a good place." It was a "knowing" which was somehow very real, and she wanted to express this to these people to whom she was so close.

"You can't talk that way!" Sandy was stopped in the middle of a sentence. An older woman that she had known well was visibly agitated and furious with her. "You can't talk like that! That's not you. It doesn't make any sense. You're too smart to say those things!"

The focus of the group switched to the woman and the therapy work became concentrated on why she was so upset. Sandy swallowed, sat back and realized that she had entered areas of life that could threaten and upset others. She sensed that the other members of her group were very glad to be able to turn to the upset woman who was acting out for all of them. They were all uncomfortable with what Sandy had been trying to say. This was different from their usual expectations of what she was like, and that unsettled them. They found it much easier to deal with her anger and her pain than this new experience. That is, everyone but Sheila. She had been sitting there quietly watching what was happening. She knew what Sandy was trying to say, for the description of recent events and feelings in Sandy's life were not so dissimilar to her own recent experiences.

As they walked to their cars, Sheila approached Sandy "I knew what you were talking about. I've had similar experiences." Sandy looked at her with relief. She had been feeling somewhat crazy. They talked briefly and found they had been reading the same books. Sheila asked Sandy if she would like to join her and their friend, Madeline, to experiment with a Ouija Board. Sheila explained how she had tried it a few times with another friend, Maryanne.

"Sure. Why don't you and Madeline come to my house on Monday evening and we'll see what happens."

Sandy knew nothing about Ouija Boards, but Jane Roberts began contacting Seth with one and that certainly turned out okay. Monday night she was ready. She bought a special notebook, arranged the living room with two facing chairs and a third for a notetaker, and made tea. Greeting the two other women, she was excited but was not really expecting anything to happen. It was all a game.

Madeline and Sheila sat at the board and Sandy took down the letters in answer to their questions. The session proceeded as follows:

Q: Is anyone there?
A: GAY BONNER   DEEFJC   WAS GAY
   BONNER,
   GOT   EFHAURTHAWAY   QGAT
   SHEILA   RUN   FWO YES

Sheila felt sure this was the same entity that she and her friend, Maryanne, had contacted a few weeks before. Sheila and Maryanne had reached this "Gay" person immediately. The messages they received were similar to those soon to follow for the three women now sitting in Sandy's living room. Sheila had found some of those messages frightening, although they later proved to be prophetic. Some of Gay's words that she then recorded in her notebook were: "LISTEN TO GAY. LONG TIME TO LISTEN. PATIENCE. JUST REACH

OUT AND U WILL NOT BE HURT. THINK FOR URSELF. CRY
HATE RAGE FEARS MOLD. UR MUCH HEALTHIER THAN
YOU BELIEVE. IT IS WITHIN U. SAY WHAT YOU THINK. CAN
HELP MANY PEOPLE RAISE THEIR BELIEFS. U HAVE TIME
BEFORE US."

Sheila did not know what these words meant. The idea of
"helping people raise their beliefs" sounded farfetched and scary. She
did feel, however, a closeness to this Gay Bonner with her cryptic,
reassuring words and began to sense what she felt was Gay's presence
in her daily meditations. She and Maryanne had about four or five
sessions with the Ouija Board and they both felt patience and encouragement from Gay, along with a sense of peace and energy. Sheila had
wanted to continue the sessions, but Maryanne was busy with a Ph.D.
dissertation and she felt she had to stop.[1] That was just the time Sandy
upset the therapy group. Now here they were, as Gay continued what
was to be the beginning of a new life for both Sandy and Sheila:

> Q: How do you know Sheila?
> A: SHEILA WAS MY SISTER
> Q: Where was Sheila your sister?
> A: WALES
> Q: Can you be more specific?
> A: DUMFERRY
> Q: What year?
> A: FRENCH WERE FIGHTING WAR
> Q: Year in figures?
> A: 1768
> Q: Was that the year Sheila was born?
> A: NO
> Q: The year you were born?
> A: YES
> Q: You were older than Sheila?
> A: NO
> Q: Parent's names?
> A: FRANCES, PETER
> Q: Last name?
> A: NO
> Q: Why not?
> A: DON'T YOU KNOW

---

[1] Madeline too later dropped out of the experiments to pursue her own activities.

She had caught them in a stupid question. She already had told them, of course, that her last name was Bonner. They learned quickly to be very precise. When they were not, she would tell them not to ask dumb questions.

Q: How did you die?
A: HEART STOPPED
Q: Heart attack?
A: YES
Q: When?
A: 1838
Q: Is there a connection with anyone else in the room?
A: SANDY
Q: Relationship to Sandy?
A: COUSIN
Q: Sandy's name at the time?
A: FRANCES
Q: Last name?
A: BONNER TOO
Q: What year was Sheila born?
A: 1750
Q: Year Sandy born?
A: 1751
Q: Were they close?
A: VERY

Chapter 2

Sheila and Sandy

THEY WERE DRIVING DOWN the Black Canyon Highway headed toward Phoenix on this last full day in Arizona before returning to Philadelphia. Sandy felt choked and had an overwhelming urge to express her feelings. She always had a harder time expressing loving feelings toward people than showing anger or irritation — especially if the person was a female. She was afraid she would cry, and she was driving.

"I want you to know that I've really appreciated this week we've spent together. I've never spent so much time with anyone before and felt so free of having to take care of their feelings."

Sheila simply said, "Yes, I know what you're saying."

They had not spoken for many miles of driving, but each had been sitting there feeling the peace that came to them with these simultaneous thoughts. It had not been the first time that day or, indeed, that week that they had found each knew what the other was thinking or feeling. Because they knew, they had been able to give each other the space and the time needed for privacy.

This week in Scottsdale was the culmination of their first nine-months experience with Gay Bonner. The three women had met once a week, talking to their "ghost," Gay, on the Ouija Board. They were mainly concerned with questions about their various and constantly changing relationships and situations. "Gay, I just met a very attractive man. Tell me if I've know him before?" or "Gay, I need a job. Where should I look?" or "My son's sick. Why?" or "What should I do about this or that?" and on and on. The questions were mundane and trivial, very much caught up in the day-to-day problems of living. The women had all discontinued their therapy sessions shortly after meeting Gay, and so their Tuesday night meetings became what they were to see later as a bridge from therapy to a new understanding of themselves. Gay patiently answered their questions, giving explanations with past-life information but always urging them to expand, to trust, to love. Sometimes she would indicate directions they could take.

"Sheila, you will be a guide for others."

"Sandy, you are a communicator and will write books instead of reading so many."

"Madeline, you can heal."

They laughed and said, "Yeah, sure!" and went about their daily lives — struggling as they always had, but sometimes they would believe her and it felt good.

Much of the material was on past lives. They didn't know what to believe about it all except that it seemed to "work." Sandy's youngest son, Griffin, from birth would become hysterical whenever he had his finger and toenails clipped. Sandy had to always hold him down as she performed this dreaded but necessary operation on her screaming, wriggling child. He was five in the early months of 1977 when, after an especially exasperating struggle, she decided to ask Gay why this was so.

A: FEAR OF A PAST LIFE
Q: When?
A: TIME OF WAR
Q: What year?
A: 1059
Q: What country?
A: France.
Q: What happened to him?
A: CAUGHT AND TORTURED
Q: How?
A: TORE OFF ALL FINGERNAILS AND TOENAILS

The next day, Sandy told Griffin about it. It couldn't get any worse, she thought. He was delighted. Instead of being frightened further, as Sandy feared, he was intrigued. He walked around for days talking about having been a soldier and having his fingernails torn out. He seemed to understand that his fear had come from that faraway time. When it became time for the next clipping, it was accomplished without the customary fight — some apprehension, but no fight. Now he nags her to do the job when his craggy nails become annoying to him.

Did Griffin "remember" on some level the pain from a past existence and react to that old memory so that conscious recall of the cause of fear lessened it? Or did the story symbolize and objectify fear so that he could psychologically better deal with it? Questions such as these continue, but whether they are ever answered objectively is less important now than it was then.

Sandy and Sheila continued reading everything they could find on the subject of reincarnation and life after death. They each continued to have "psychic" experiences – feelings for Sheila; visual glimpses for Sandy. In April of 1977, Sandy read Dick Sutphen's *You Were Born Again to be Together* – a book she had rejected because of its title and cover as being "another one of those books" until Sheila, who had read it a year or so before, recommended it. (Sheila read books much differently than Sandy. She seems to breathe them in, often without conscious thought or intellectual scrutiny. She may begin a book in the middle or at the end, moving backwards, or forward and backward at the same time. After she has read it, if it has been important to her, she will absorb its content and it has become a part of her. She does this quietly and without much fanfare. Sandy, on the other hand, begins on page one, examines every sentence for intellectual integrity, makes judgments as to worth, and broadcasts the results as she progresses.) She read a third of Sutphen's book in one afternoon while at work, rushed home, called Sheila, and announced: "We're going to Scottsdale."

The trip to Scottsdale was another major turning point in their lives and their relationship. The feelings each were having on the Black Canyon Highway that day in July were the basis of what was to be a new working relationship – a relationship that would create a psychic bond between them so strong that, without each having a strong and individual sense of self, could evolve into unbalanced dependencies with ensuing resentment and hostility. That day had come at the end of an intense week of learning.

Dick Sutphen not only writes books but also conducts seminars, and that year his July seminar was designed to give its participants direct experience with their past lives through regressive hypnosis. What had excited Sandy when she read the book was Dick's confirmation of the kind of material they had been getting from Gay. This was important for them, as they had learned very quickly that their explorations with Gay were considered threatening, and sometimes even evil, by many of the people around them – their friends and co-workers. They had, because of these reactions, "gone into the closet" with their activities, telling no one what they were doing. Consequently, they had no outside feedback or confirmation of their material, other than through their reading, and many of the books found in the occult section of bookstores seemed silly and sensational to them.

The events and people Sandy and Sheila experienced while in Scottsdale that July pulled them out of their claustrophobic closet and pushed them onto new paths, leading in directions they had never considered before. Those people and events will turn up throughout this book. Important here is the growing awareness in the two women of a special closeness that was freeing, while intimate, and would be significant later on.

During that week in Scottsdale, their movements through the various events seemed orchestrated, designed in such a way that their interrelatedness glided with the ease of well-oiled bearings. They moved together when they felt together or when each needed space to be — to talk or not to talk, to be alone or not to be alone, to sleep or to run, to read or to meditate, to cry or to laugh. They never seemed to get in each other's way, never felt the need to do other than that which each wanted to do in order to "take care of" the other's feelings or needs.

This specialness in their relating continued after they returned from Arizona, and their work began in earnest. As time passed, they began to realize more and more the "coincidences" of their lives. Their mothers had the same name and similar personalities. Neither lived close to their families. Both had moved to the area in which they lived now, after several moves around the East Coast. Relationships with people in their lives followed similar patterns. Each took turns being first in a learning situation, so that understanding and emotional support flowed equally and easily from one to the other. They were continually surprised to find they had experienced the same feelings at different times, so both had the benefit of "knowing" intimately a specific kind of learning.

First there was Skip. Sheila began seeing him in October, just as she and Sandy were starting their new business, Mind Matters, and beginning to realize their serious commitment to a working relationship that would be interdependent, and because of its intimacy, based on trust. Skip wanted to be married. He wanted a conventional marriage with a home and children. He was thirty years old and had never married. It was time, and he fell in love with Sheila. Now, at first this was fine. He was quite supportive of her interest in the psychic world, of her regular meetings with Sandy, and of the few readings they had started doing. Soon, however, Sheila's time away from him began to chafe. "You're always at Sandy's." Sandy felt his resentment. She began to realize that he saw what they were doing as a lark, as fun and games, and that he had "serious" business with Sheila. She got scared. At first, she did not want to say anything about her fears. After all, it was Sheila's business to be with whom she pleased. That non-interference in each other's lives was an important part of their relating.

Her fears began building and she imagined "losing" Sheila. She was sure the man, because he was a man, would take away her friend and their work together. When the pressure became unbearable, she finally articulated her fears. Sheila listened quietly. She did not protest, deny Sandy's feelings, or call her crazy. She listened and said she understood.

"It's true that it's what he wants from me," Sheila said, "and you're feeling his resentment and anger because it's not what I want. I want to do our work together as it evolves. If he can't take it seriously, then that's his problem."

Relief. Everything was back in perspective. Their work grew and Sheila's relationship with Skip died of its own natural causes.

The following summer, the situation reversed. Sandy became intensely involved with a yoga instructor – a passionately dedicated student of Eastern philosophies. For a number of months, Sandy was as passionately dedicated to him as he was to his ideas. She practiced yoga, meditated "religiously," talked of rising above the "trash" of the world to gain enlightenment, and worst of all, repeated to Sheila the man's talk of psychic phenomena being "bad" because it distracted one from the true and only meaningful path to "real" spirituality. She read his books and listened to him put hers down as less than spiritual. Sheila became alarmed. Was Sandy taking all this as seriously as she appeared to? Would she decide their work with Gay and with psychic development was "trash?" Would she take a vow of poverty and chastity and disappear into an ashram to "Pursue the Path to Enlightenment?" Sheila could see she cared very much for the man and that she was learning a great deal from the relationship. She felt that it was not her business to interfere if Sandy were to choose a new direction. Her fears built, and there was a strain growing between them. Finally, Sheila spoke about her feelings.

"That's how I felt about you and Skip!" They laughed, talked, and knew it was okay. Sandy's involvement in Eastern disciplines was not what it had appeared to be to Sheila; and a couple of months later, the intensely passionate attraction to the man ended with an intensely passionate explosion.

Sometimes in their struggles with men, Gay would say to them, "You make it much too difficult. It's all much simpler than you make it." Both examined their beliefs regarding work and men and, like many women in their culture, found that they believed the two were incompatible. If they were to do serious and meaningful work, they would have to forego intimate and close relationships with men. If they chose men, home and children, then creative, independent work was out of the question. They were afraid then of "commitment," for commitment meant a "giving up" or giving over of oneself to another — a man — who would then have claims on their energy as well as their time and talents. They found they believed all men needed to be taken care of — needed to have their egos soothed and nursed — and at their expense. This, they felt, had been their experience, and so that was the way it was. Gay kept telling them otherwise. "*You* are committed to each other, and yet you are free. Why can't you allow this with men?"

It sounded simple enough. It was true with them. When misunderstanding or disagreement occurred, they easily talked about their feelings; and the talking took care of the problem. They made their own decisions about what they wanted to do, and then did it, without feeling as if they "had to," say, go to a movie or a party — if that was what the other "wanted." They each had their own friends and social interests, and there was never a question that Sheila should spend time with someone because Sandy wanted her to do so, or that Sandy should be at a certain place because Sheila insisted on it. They were free in their relating, yet committed to each other as supportive, loving friends and business partners. Why then could this not happen in all their relationships?

"Let things just be," Gay would tell them. "Give up and let go." A paradox resided in that action, for they would find that when they did "give up," they would usually get what they wanted. Gay spoke to them again about commitment — this time in regard to a long-time relationship of Sandy's — but as usual, the words applied to their entire lives:

> Actually you humans on a physical level do not understand commitment. Commitment is not something you decide. It is not even static or fixed or permanent. It is or is not. You are both already committed anyway. The bond is there, and there are no big decisions to make. The fear is in admitting that you are committed now. Saying this for you both implies that it is forever and chains are around you. You both believe because of past experiences that it will mean unhappiness and dishonesty....It need not mean

chains, unhappiness, dishonesty or loss of freedom. It can be liberating, but up to you. I am not predicting anything but only explaining commitment. Commitment is not a promise, a vow. It is a psychic bond and simply exists or does not. When it does not, you will both know and be ready for new experiences. When it does, simply enjoy and love. Very simple.

Chapter 3

Who is Gay Bonner?

IN A PRIVATE SESSION with Gay on August 5, 1977, Sandy asked the following questions:

Q: What is your relationship to Sheila? Sheila is sometimes confused because her thoughts "feel" like yours.

A: I am the you who refuses to face all the power, and I am the knowing part of you.

Q: Are you also Gay Bonner who lived in 18th Century Wales?

A: I am also Gay Bonner, and those were to be my next words. Do you see? We are one, yet two or sometimes three or four. In life we were meeting as one – then we split.

Q: You were coming from the same source?

A: As we all. We came so close as to be one person.

Q: You and Sheila?

A: Yes.

Q: In the life in the 1700s you were two?

A: Now we are two.

Q: Was that the life where you split?

A: I don't see the question.

Q: Was the Wales life the first life where you and Sheila split into two persons?

A: After the end of being one, we were two.

Q: I'm confused. Am I asking a "time" question?

A: There is confusion. Read later the notes – that it is possible to be two in one then later two separate and back again, if we choose.

The questions and resulting confusion during this relatively early session with Gay were typical during those times. Gay had been speaking through Sheila's body regularly since their trip to Scottsdale the month before. Much later, they began to realize that Gay speaks to them literally, completely out of the present moment. She and Sheila become one when she is speaking through Sheila's body. Then they become two when she returns to whatever reality she comes from, and Sheila becomes fully physical again. Later in the same session, she talked further about how she relates to Sheila, as well as to Madeline and Sandy. She also spoke about herself, her feelings and her preferences.

Gay: I have been around, and she (Sheila) didn't choose to have a relationship with me.

Q: You chose it?

Gay: We both did.

Q: Earlier than this?

Gay: Only when she was six years old. I was there, and we spoke.

Q: In physical life?

Gay: No, spirit form, and we spoke. She has no memory of spirit friends. She was laughed at for talking to herself.

Q: You left her until now?

Gay: I had no choice. I did stand by in dreams and fantasies.

Q: How do you relate to Madeline and me?

Gay: I have been with you two, and I am your guide also.

Q: But the relationship is not as intimate as it is with Sheila?

Gay: No, but it is close.

Q: Can you tell us about some of your other physical lives (other than the one in Wales, where we knew her)?

Gay: My other physical lives have been many. I was in Athens. A female. I occupied no particular place (position in society). Usually I have always been observing and taking in. I'm not a very physical being. I never really fit into a body very well at all. My lives were really not significant in your earth terms. Most of my work has been in Arcadia[1] and Atlantis — and also in ASC (spelled out).[2]

Q: Were you a physical person in Atlantis?

Gay: No. I was your spirit; however, I was known to all there.

Q: Did the people in Atlantis have more access to the spirit world than we do?

Gay: Just the same. You are beginning to use almost as much.

---

[1] According to Gay, Arcadia is a spiritual place of rest between lives.

[2] Perhaps "altered states of consciousness?" This was not pursued at the time, nor since.

On September 13, 1977, she tried again to help us understand how we relate. We were still not seeing that her words were literal and spoken from a present, here and now, perspective.

Gay: The relationship is one that I am a part of you, and you (Sandy and Madeline) and we were one.

Q: The three of us were one?

Gay: No. I was you and you and am Sheila...you can feel me in part of you still – in your thoughts and writing. I would really like for you to understand more, but sometimes I search for words, and there are none that you would understand if I used them; so I and you are limited...you see, what I was referring to about the closeness was the actual taking over of her body now, but I'm as close to you with your thoughts, dreams, writing.

Q: Could Madeline and I do what Sheila does and allow you to speak through our bodies?

Gay: If you believe, yes, you could. Your problem would just be in a disbelief, but the information is all available anyway. One way is no different really. This (Sheila in trance) is just more convenient.

Who or what is Gay Bonner? During the first months that the two women met with her, they questioned little about the nature of the communication they had established. Gay Bonner was simply a sister and cousin in a past life they had lived in 18th Century Wales. As they grew more sophisticated in their understanding of the metaphysical world, their questions changed and the answers became less conventional and traditionally simple.

While in Scottsdale, Sandy and Sheila met David and Linda Paladin. David Paladin is an Anglo-Indian raised by his mother's Navajo people. Spirits and other worldly communications were commonplace during his childhood. And now, in his adult life, David is a psychic channel who speaks for several "spooks," as he and Linda call them. David has been written about extensively by Dick Sutphen and also by Alan Weisman in *We, Immortals.* He has also been the subject of numerous magazine and newspaper articles. He was a featured speaker at Dick's seminar that July.

During the seminar, Sheila and Sandy kept pretty much to themselves. They told no one about their communications with Gay. They were still using the Ouija Board, although Sheila had spoken directly for Gay for a short period of time during the latter months of 1976. She had become quite sick and frightened by it. She insisted that they return to using the Board. They decided to take a chance and talk to David and Linda about Gay and their feelings and fears.

Their meeting with David and Linda was an immediate disappointment. They left the room wondering exactly what had happened and why they had gone there. It seemed to them that David had talked a great deal about himself, rambling about his experiences, while Linda continually urged him back to the two women before him and their questions. Little did they realize the effect David and his "spooks" were to have on their lives. At the time, they did not "take in" what he was saying. Everything seemed like a lot of words – general advice and reassurance. David said he felt good about Gay. He seemed to "know" her and reassured Sheila and Sandy that her intentions were positive. This seemed to them very vague and non-specific as they walked back to their room fuming about the encounter. However, as soon as they reached their hotel room, Sheila laid down on the couch and began speaking for Gay. This was the beginning of a new phase in their relationship to Gay and the work they would do with her. A year later, David and Linda would visit them in Philadelphia. They learned then the full extent of David's influence and much about a "higher self" communication that occurs on a different level of consciousness. There Gay – or the "Gay Bonner" parts of their consciousness – communicates with David's "spooks," causing a positive influence and encouragement to filter directly down to them at their level of normal consciousness.

David had suggested that they ask Gay what she wanted from them. That had never occurred to them before. For nine months, she had patiently answered their questions and urged them toward self-confidence in their talents. She had continually pressed them to accept their worthiness and beauty and to set aside their self-doubts and negative self-judgment. When they asked what she wanted of them, however, the material immediately changed, becoming abstract and metaphysical. For instance, she insisted that they "move to her." Sandy asked how.

Gay: You have come here with me again tonight. First I want to say I, too, search. Who am I? Who are you? We are the same. That's the question for all.

Q: Do you have all the answers or do you have a guide? How do you know what to say?

Gay: I see from a different perspective and tell you that I have no answers. You have all the answers. You have no answers. I have all answers. We only tell each other our perspective.

Q: What do you want?

Gay: I want to experience your lives too. Share with me more than just problems.

Q: As we experience, you do too?

Gay: Yes. Share with me more. I want to experience more adventure. Thank you.

Q: Can you communicate with three people at once? (Sandy had in mind that Gay had said that she was a guide for Sheila, Madeline and herself.)

Gay: All of this is "at once." I say all at once. Since you think of last year — let's say, 1976, your time, I say (she whistled a long blowing sound). Here it is. Take it as you are ready. I can do same with space. Pull it out of time, out of space. Your words somewhat limit me.

Later, when they began doing readings for other people, Sheila and Sandy began to appreciate what Gay was trying to teach them. Since they had had no knowledge of mediums or psychics until their own experiences began, they had no intellectual base for what was happening. Later, they were to read in Lawrence LeShan's *The Medium, the Mystic, and the Physicist:*

> In the Clairvoyant Reality (the reality from which the medium speaks)…time takes on quite a different structure [than Sensory Reality, where time flows at a steady pace in one direction]. The past, the present, and the future are all equally in existence, even though we can ordinarily only observe those events located in the present. It is as if one were describing what happens when a movie is being shown. All the events of the movie are in existence: they are on the celluloid film already, but we can only see a very narrow slice of the film at any one time. As the frames of the film pass behind the lens of the projector and flash on the screen it looks to us as if the events were happening, but in reality the entire film and all the events on it (…) already exist. (Page 36.)

So what or who is Gay Bonner? The more the two women learned, the more questions and theories they encountered. She was no longer a simple reincarnational relative speaking to them from the "other side," wherever that may be. Gay could pull information out of time and space. Her perspective on their lives had certainly given them valuable, insightful help and was soon to do the same for many others. Questions kept coming up.

During a session in November of 1977, Gay told Sheila that she gave her more than she would ever realize. Sandy asked Gay what she got from the exchange.

Gay: You give me a chance to do my work and talk to people. I enjoy coming to you and you come to me. This is just as valuable for me to learn also by observing more closely your lives. This is my work and yours...we are all involved in learning. Some of us are here to guide; others are, in your case, to teach and show others. Once we find our work, we also tend to grow.

After Sheila and Sandy returned from Scottsdale, Gay began talking to other people. The trip to Arizona gave them courage to speak out and gradually let others know what they were doing. The people they met there – Dick and Trenna Sutphin, David and Linda Paladin, Brad Steiger and his soon-to-be wife Francie, as well as a couple of hundred regular, middle-class men and women – had experienced psychic events similar to those they had been having during the past nine months. They were not crazy or weird, or flirting with dangerous unknown evils. Spiritual and psychic matters were more open in the clear, dry desert air than in beautifully green, conservative Bucks County, Pennsylvania. As they opened, however, they soon were to find others like themselves who were discovering new and exciting parts of their whole beings.

They began with friends. A friend of Sandy's, in emotional turmoil over the end of her marriage, was the first to come. She had not worked in years and now wanted some kind of career direction. Her major in college had been art – ceramics in particular. Sandy asked Gay if she would speak to her friend. "Yes, I have something to say to her, if she wants, to guide her life. I'm anxious to meet her...I will guide for awhile, and she can jump out of the pots, not into the frying pan."

The friend came and left with a new direction to her life. The next friend to speak to Gay was a friend of Sheila's. He was separated from his wife. He asked Gay why he had such a need to take care of his wife and why she resented it so much. This was one of the basic difficulties they had. Gay told him that his wife had been his mentally retarded child in a previous lifetime. Now she wanted him to see that she could care for herself, understand him and be understood by him. He told his wife what Gay had said. Sandy and Sheila panicked. The wife called. "How did you know how I've always felt? All my life I've had a fear of mental retardation." She too came and talked to Gay. Now she, her husband, and their young son come periodically to talk to Gay. The number of people coming grew. One person would tell someone else, and so on. Sheila and Sandy soon found themselves conducting a business. Gay had "gone public."

The question of who she is became even more complex, and yet the two women were gaining an intuitive understanding of the process that will perhaps never be definitively explained in a normal, rational, and logical mode of consciousness. Is Sheila's subconscious tapping into a universal consciousness personified as Gay Bonner?

Sandy had lunch with a psychiatrist who approached life with a traditional psychoanalytic point of view. As she explained to him what happened when Sheila laid on her couch and began talking in a different voice with a different personality, he leaned across the table toward her, tension mounting in his body. Suddenly he fell back into his chair exclaiming, "Oh well, we have several cases of split personalities at the hospital." He was satisfied with his diagnosis. Sandy simply looked at him and attempted no defense. She knew her friend wasn't "crazy."

Jung's theory of a collective unconscious offered one explanation. Perhaps Sheila could go beyond her usual rational consciousness to delve into a deeper clairvoyant reality where all thoughts and ideas "exist," in order to pull up that information, and present it by a "spirit" people would listen to.

Other people's questions added to their understanding of the process. In October, 1978, they held a group session with several people interested in asking philosophical questions, rather than the usual personal ones. One man jokingly asked. "Gay, what turns you on?" Her answer was long and presented them with new thoughts, not only about who she was but who they were:

Gay: I have always had a curiosity and an interest in how people behave and relate to each other, their environment – physical environment, mental environment, and the spiritual environment. It is this curiosity that I have that, in a sense, "turns me on." Actually I was initially "turned on" by Shelia's interest. It seemed to intersect and then be all of you. Remember, I am a thought form created by you all here, and I am involved in your interests also. In the realm that my thoughts exist, I also do listen to beautiful music and enjoy creating scenes that are perfect works of art, and I can "read" any literature I so choose. This I enjoy, but you are thinking and perceiving me as a person also and so sometimes communication is difficult, but this is the only way for now. I like talking to people, and I have arranged this because I wish to be in both worlds at once. You can also live in both worlds at once, but not consciously doing so. This is a conscious exchange. Both Sheila and I wanted to try this, and the exchange is exciting in itself, for we both know who we are; but we can have fun of being and experiencing someone else also. This is often done, but we are choosing to do it at a more conscious level. It is quite fascinating to make this switch also.

Q: Aren't you a person?

Gay: Yes, I am in one sense, but you also are a person and need to be conscious of that fact too.

A: You mean flesh and blood person?

Gay: Yes.

Q: But are you Gay Bonner with past lives and also a "thought form"?

Gay: You both (Sandy and Sheila) gave me my name and lives.

Q: Explain that please.

Gay: You create me and made my history also.

Q: Are you independent from us at all?

Gay: That is a question of considerable thought and requires an answer that may seem difficult to understand. It is not possible for me to be independent of you.

Q: But I (Sandy) am independent of Bob sitting here next to me?

Gay: You may very well feel that way if you choose, but you are not independent.

Q: You mean that when he leaves I will be different?

Gay: Yes.

Q: Are each of us thought forms as you?

Gay: Yes, and you are people too, which means that you are also responsible for a physical existence.

Q: We choose physical bodies and their limitations?

Gay: Yes, but become sometime totally your bodies and then you will become your spirit also.

Q: What do you mean?

Gay: Feel them.

Q: How?

Gay: You need to just be aware of them.

Q: In a different way than normally?

Gay: You normally are not.

In march of 1979, speaking to an ESP class that Sheila was conducting, Gay said the following:

> You all have greater souls and power. Your guides are connected psychically and, as such, represent the wise parts of yourself. They are not magic or mysterious. I had certain thoughts and ideas expressed many times in physical form. Sheila and I have similar

deep beliefs and outlooks so, of course, we would meet psychically. It is easier and material is greater when we combine energies.
I am not separate. Sheila is not separate. Even two people meeting
on a physical plane having a conversation are not separate. They
join energies to create a piece of communication. That is all.

Gay was now calling herself a thought form created by those
speaking to her. At the same time, on a different level of understanding
now, she presented herself as a distinct and different personality with
her own experience and being apart from others. The material on who
she is became much more mystical in nature. She was telling them that
they and they alone created everything in their lives, including the
people they experienced and the events in which they participated. She
was telling them this in a gradual manner, which made an intuitive
understanding of these ideas possible. They had recognized these ideas
intellectually when they had read Jane Roberts' books, but it was Gay
who, day by day, taught them intuitive knowing.

On October 21, 1978, she answered another of the group's
questions. They asked if she had any rules that dictate her existence?
Any limits set by her or higher beings as to what she could tell them?
They also asked for her after-death impressions.

First, there are no rules for my existence, just as there are none for
yours. Any limitations are self imposed. You contribute even to
my limitations as I contribute to yours. This is because we are one.
What I say is what you can hear at any given moment. That is the
way it operates always. That is, not that there are things I can't tell
you, only things you do not hear. You know everything anyway. I
can say nothing new. All laws can be transcended. Even natural
laws can be transcended in other "realities" that you are free to
enter at any given time. You have chosen to operate within a given
framework of existence. So do I. There is no being beyond yourself. You are the dictator and ruler for yourself. Any forces that
appear outside of you have been placed there in order that you
may feel more comfortable than you would if you realized they are
you....The tour of conditions after death would be only what I
encountered. There are millions of after-death conditions, just as
there are millions of physical life conditions...I found it different
each time I died. I will explain what it is like now for me. I sense
much more vividly the feelings of the surroundings, and I seem to
have a way of feeling the universe. I do not see, but feel and hear.
This is my own particular way. There are indeed levels.
Remember, levels here are not meaning better or higher, but exist
side by side. It is a tone like a musical vibration. Many different

tones and notes together making the total composition – same
with the universe.

In the Fall of 1978, Jane Roberts published *The Afterdeath
Journal of an American Philosopher: The Worldview of William
James*. James, through Jane Roberts, had this to say about his after-
death perspective.

> If sharpness of detail is lost, I am quite able to follow large pat-
> terns of thought and emotions with ease, perceiving them some-
> what above the hard-bed reality of the world, rising from it like
> multicolored clouds of different shapes, colors, and varieties. All
> in all, then, I can follow the world's ideas and emotional climate
> very well. Realities connected with your own experience, but
> invisible to you, are quite clear from my viewpoint, then, while
> ordinary events of a physical nature are unclear and shadowy.
>
> I can follow thoughts' masses as they form above the
> world, mixing with others, flowing in patterns sometimes light,
> sometimes dark or dimming, and I can perceive the intensity of
> emotion that drives them. As a rain cloud will surely bring a
> shower, from my standpoint it is obvious that certain thought
> patterns will bring about physical events suiting their nature; so it
> is with considerable interest that I watch those emotional and
> mental patterns that surround the world. (Page 119.)

Gay repeatedly insists that her words are another perspective
and should be taken only as that. This perspective comes from another
state of consciousness that sees "large patterns of thought and emotions," patterns we lose as we are caught in "the hard-bed reality of the
world," with its immediate, concrete detail. As we become more and
more aware of the multilayered nature of our total being, this perspective, this consciousness is more readily accessible to us – whether we
consult personified guides such as Gay, or delve into the layers of our
minds through meditation, or simply learn to watch our thoughts and
to distinguish those that come to us from various levels of our being.

Chapter 4

Experiencing Gay

SHEILA'S BODY LAY on the bed. Sandy was sitting next to her taking notes, while Gay spoke. The two women were in Scottsdale, Arizona, for the second time this early morning in October of 1977. As Sandy recorded Gay's words, she became concerned by the deliberate, almost painful, slowness of her delivery. The words came haltingly, with a more pronounced distortion of Sheila's facial features than usual. Worried that something was wrong, Sandy stopped Gay and asked if there was some difficulty in coming through? Was she too far away to communicate easily?

Gay: I am actually more here than there. When I totally take over, sometimes it is more difficult.

Sandy: This is one of those times?

Gay: Yes.

Sandy: You are far away?

Gay: No, I'm closer.

Sandy: You mean you are more in Sheila's body than usual?

Gay: Yes. Sometimes she aids me. Sometimes she is off exploring other realities.

Sandy: Is this one of those times?

Gay: Yes.

Sandy: Can she remember where she goes?

Gay: She doesn't want to believe that, as now she is listening to me from a distance and sometimes she even doubts this. She claims she never leaves her body.

Sandy: Is that why this experience has been more real for me than for her?

Gay: Yes, you can see she is gone. Do you sense it more now?

Sandy: Yes. That's why I asked. I knew something was wrong or different because you spoke so slowly and deliberately.

Gay: I'm working hard, and I would like to show her more, but I take this gradually because there is much time.

Sandy: Will we get more conscious understanding of the process as we proceed?

Gay: Yes. She feels she is standing behind my voice. Actually, she is out just observing and exploring. Sometime she will write it down but now does not even believe it.

Just as Gay finished those words, Sheila's body jerked and jumped on the bed. Her eyes were fluttering quickly and a few seconds later she opened her eyes and was back. A fly had landed on her mouth, startling her out of the trance. The exchange was the fastest and most dramatic Sandy had witnessed since Sheila began talking for Gay regularly the previous July.

"Sheila, I'm sorry," Sandy exclaimed. "I've been nagging and berating you for months now about your doubts around Gay, her existence and her validity. Now I realize that you've never experienced her directly. You're always off somewhere."

This had been a point of contention between them. Sandy never could understand why Sheila had so many doubts and questions. During those early days, Sheila would become discouraged and often insist that Gay was not real, or that Gay did not know what she was doing. Before sessions, Sheila would be very skeptical, afraid that Gay would not come through, or that she would botch it, telling people things that would upset them or that meant nothing to them. Sandy seldom felt that way. She would protest Sheila's complaints and say, "But how can you doubt after all that's happened?"

On this clear Arizona morning, Sandy gained some empathy for her friend. Sheila was not there when Gay was. Sandy experienced the change in voice, facial expression and personality when Gay was speaking. To her, Gay Bonner's existence was a concrete, sensually perceived experience. Gay was simply not Sheila. Her voice was deeper. Her facial expressions more emphatic. Her diction more cadenced. Her vocabulary different. Her syntax often tortuous. Her presence insistent and forceful. Gay commands attention with a quiet forcefulness and energy that pulls the consciousness of those hearing her into a trance-like concentration. She speaks without punctuation, her words pouring out in a stream of thought that often interweaves several meanings and ideas into one long paragraph. The person she is addressing often reports knowing a "meaning" that is far deeper than the words she has spoken. Sandy experiences that "knowing" frequently during their private sessions — some understanding of the material that is deeper than the words imply. People often report a sense of energy being exchanged between Gay and themselves when she is speaking directly to them. This "energy" in some way adds to the meaning of the words and the sense of positive well-being people usually feel after talking to her.

All of this experience had given Sandy a certainty about what they were doing. Sheila was not sure.

When they had first started communicating with Gay and were using the Ouija Board, they found that Sheila's participation on the board was necessary for the words to come through clearly. Gay said it was due to closeness between Sheila and herself. That closeness improved the energy, she said. Madeline and Sandy could take turns on the other side of the board, but Sheila was needed to contact Gay. Soon after they began, Sheila started feeling a band of pressure around her head, circling it like an Indian headband. When she started experiencing this, she also found that she could anticipate the words coming across the board. She began to wonder if she were guiding the pointer, although the answers were often different than what her own conscious answers would have been to the same questions. The words were somehow entering her mind but were not consciously "thought up." At first, only the word coming across would pop into her head, but soon whole phrases and sentences were there before the slow pointer of the board would spell them out.

After a few weeks, she and Madeline were having a session in her apartment. The board spelled out "GET OFF THE BOARD." Sheila then began speaking for Gay. Excited, all three women thought they were finished with the slow, ponderous board. For several weeks Sheila spoke for Gay. For the most part, the material during that time was general and reassuring. If Sandy or Madeline asked Gay a specific question, either Sheila would come out of trance or the answer would be general. Gay reassured them that they were progressing. Sheila was getting in touch with her talent and her power.

Sheila felt wonderful. It was as if she had been catapulted to a beautiful new consciousness. She wanted to stay there. She was high and the world was lovely and exciting. People responded to her new awareness, seeing her beauty and her power.

Her high was not to last. The pain started, and by December she was in Pennsylvania Hospital with a severe infection. She knew emotional pain, but this was different. Until now, her life had been relatively free of physical pain; but on December 1st, 1976, she wrote the following in her journal: "Across my belly, like a knife cutting in me. I say I can't stand any more and try to avoid feeling it, but I know I must...someone please help me!" The pain lasted for a couple of months. The sessions stopped for a while, and when they began again Sheila insisted on returning to the board for communication with Gay. She had associated her illness with speaking for Gay.

Much later, Sheila was able to see that she had had a lot of fear about what was happening to her — childhood religious fears of possession; adult psychological fears of being controlled by another. She also found that she continued to have a need to hide her talents and powers. If others found out that she had abilities and was more than "dumb, sweet Sheila" — the image she had publicly presented as a defense since her childhood — then they were not going to like her, or they would think she was crazy. These fears manifested as physical illness. Slowly and carefully now, she examined her beliefs and fears, and by the time she and Sandy met David Paladin in July, she was ready to begin using the talents that were uniquely hers.

During those months, she continually received encouragement from Gay and support from Sandy and Madeline. In March, 1977, she wrote of her struggle in her journal. "In trance tonight. Felt the familiar numbness — head, hands, fingers, feet — and I know the words were: 'No way will I let you in, Gay. NO NO NO'. Fear she will control me if I let her in. Realized for the first time what's been happening. I won't let her in. I do go to her! But only so far."

At a later time, Gay reassured her:

> You come to me. Perfectly natural. Don't be afraid of natural happenings. You moved. You believe! Otherwise you wouldn't be here. See, you are not crazy. Don't act dumb — I mean that in the sense you say "crazy, weird, strange"...it's very natural. Keep going. It's almost like you can't go fast enough. Do you want me to slow down?

Gay's last words reflected Sheila's ambivalence. She wanted the relationship with Gay and wanted it immediately. At the same time she feared it. Eventually she and Gay worked out an agreement. Gay would come into her consciousness and body only when Sheila invited her. This arrangement suited Sheila, and much of the confusion about which thoughts were hers (Sheila's) and which were Gay's abated. Later Sheila would become able to recognize immediately "Gay in her head," and her own thoughts and impressions. As she became comfortable with the situation, her own sense of identity strengthened, and she was able to accept Gay as a part of herself as well as a separate being whom she had been resisting.

After her marriage ended, Sheila had taken a new name—Sheila Ilona Reynolds. The initials SIR had been psychologically important to her at the time. She was coming in touch with her own strength — what she saw as the masculine part of herself. In April of 1978, she was able to introduce Gay into the totality of her being. She wrote the following in her journal: "I'm not afraid of anything. Sometimes it seems like I am because I've forgotten about the SIR of me. From now on I'll call the 'knowing' part of me SIR. It's strong and masculine and unafraid. There's me, Sheila (which is OK, too), but Sheila forgets about SIR and SIR's help. Then there is Gay. I'm not sure exactly what Gay is besides a guide to me and others, but SIR trusts Gay much more than Sheila. So there are three sides to me, or parts to me, really. I do know there is one Whole Me, but it seems to come out in three parts. I'm not sure where SIR, Gay and Sheila fit into these parts, but I do know when I begin to think of these three, I feel whole again, like man, woman, and yet a blending of both."

Sandy had her doubts as well. She could accept the personality she knew as Gay when she was speaking through Sheila's body. She had a harder time accepting that she, too, had access to the same information — the same collective unconscious. She had to learn to accept that she had a "Gay" within her consciousness, and that she too could communicate directly with her. Soon after they started with Gay, she found that if she would put herself into a light trance, ask questions with a pen and paper, answers soon would come. Her first attempts were mostly squiggly lines slanting across the paper, usually quite unintelligible. She insisted on keeping her eyes closed and "making" the pen move itself, without any interference from her. Somehow, under those rigid circumstances, she did occasionally receive information. Usually she did not trust it. After making an attempt, she would wait until Sheila had a session, ask Gay directly the same question, and most often, would receive the same answer! Sometimes even the words were the same, but usually the sense agreed with her automatic writing. Along with these messages, Gay would exhort her to trust her mind and allow her impressions to flow. After returning from Arizona that July, she too found a new confidence. She allowed the automatic writing to happen. She would sit with pen and paper, or at the typewriter, and let her stream of consciousness flow with whatever was on her mind — usually some kind of problem or emotional crisis in her daily life. As she would write, she would suddenly notice that the "I" she had been writing switched to "You," and the answers would flow onto the paper. The words would feel as if they simply "appeared" and sometimes would not make sense until she read what they said later. She found that the answers were also helpful and began to accept that they were indeed from Gay. But whose Gay? Was her Gay the same Gay that spoke through Sheila? Were both women tapping into a "thought form" or a collection of thoughts they called Gay Bonner? The same questions kept coming up, and still do. There are several answers, as were discussed in Chapter 3, but both women feel that any attempt to define the process by claiming one answer as "truth" would limit the potential for exploration.

The psychic bond created between Sandy and Sheila, because of their work, explains the kind of telepathy that often occurs between them and between their own "Gay parts," their higher selves. An empathy between the two women, which exists even when they are apart, often makes possible a knowledge of each other's moods. Sometimes the "knowing" is very concrete.

In August, 1977, Sheila was still working for the Pennsylvania Board of Assistance. The training job she had been doing was dissolved and Sheila did not know where her supervisors would place her within the welfare office. She knew that she did not want to return to a caseworker's position. This had happened to her co-trainer and seemed to be the only alternative. During some automatic writing that Sandy had been receiving on a problem she had at the time, Gay (her Gay?) said the following for Sheila:

> On Sheila's job. She will not be there very long anyway, and what time left will be easy. She doesn't have to experience a caseload. That is important for her to know.

Sandy called Sheila and read to her what Gay had said. Immediately after Sandy read the message, Sheila's boss walked into her office and told her that she may not have to carry a caseload after all. Several days later she was given a supervisory position much more to her liking. She left the welfare office to work full time with psychic matters in February of 1978, five months later, just after she and Sandy started Mind Matters.

One young man who Gay particularly seemed to like returned for his second reading. (Sandy always knows when Gay prefers a particular person. She behaves positively toward all coming with questions but, once in a while, Sandy senses a "specialness" in the way she relates to certain people.) After leaving his first reading, Smitty continued to feel "high" and experienced a great deal of energy. He asked about this now:

Gay: You indeed felt my presence and energy, just as you are now. This is indeed real…I like you very much; so when you left from talking to me before, the energy you took was real; but you let it go when you began to question it…

Smitty: Gay, will you go out on a date with me?

Gay: It is possible to spend some time with you as this would involve thoughts to me, then I could share in your view of the world. Sometimes I do anyway, when you think of me or when thoughts of you are transmitted to this level here; and so in that respect, we can share and exchange much. You can view my world too. I am only a thought form. I have not yet chosen to explore this particular year in physical form, but can get a world view from your perspective also. Sometimes you can do this too. You can tap into someone else's perspective and see from their viewpoint. Do this even better by first going into a trance…

Later, when Smitty showed a reluctance to ask her direct questions, she said:

> You need not hesitate to talk.…Although you cannot physically see me, my thoughts are being put through this woman here.

Gay certainly seemed to expand beyond the perimeters of Sheila's consciousness. Smitty could and had experienced her energy and "presence" after leaving Sheila's presence. This kind of experience is often reported by people who come for sessions. Sometimes the energy is felt emotionally — "almost overwhelming feelings of love for the world," as one man put it. Other times people report simply feeling "good" or "high." Others experience bursts of creative energy, and whatever work they are currently doing seems to flow easier.

The sessions had a consistent format that grew out of the first few readings and became the guide for others. People could, of course, ask any questions they wished, but most asked questions that generally fell into four main areas: their relationships, their talents and abilities, their beliefs — especially beliefs limiting their full potential as creative beings — and their spiritual growth. Usually Sandy and Sheila would ask that the person coming think about and write down questions of concern in those areas. They did not know why they asked this, but realized that it gave Sheila confidence and something to concentrate on as she went into trance. Typically, when a new client arrives for a reading, the two women serve tea, discuss the questions, explain what is going to happen, and then Sheila lies down and begins to breathe deeply. For several seconds of quiet, Sheila breathes, Sandy concentrates on Gay's name, and usually the client, especially if he or she is new to the experience, stops breathing. Then Gay begins. There is no other ritual. No candles, no low lights or incense. Often the television can be heard upstairs in Sandy's house, her children giggling or talking in response to it or their own games.

Gay speaks in blocks of words, often without punctuation, usually interweaving several answers into a continuous stream of thought. Her voice is lower than Sheila's, and is even in tone, displaying little if any emotion. She relates the material in a matter-of-fact manner, devoid of judgment or embellishment. Her often-stated goal in the readings is to bring people in touch with their personal power, their beauty, and potential. Her message is that they, and they alone, create their lives in whatever manner they choose in order to learn and grow. Sometimes, they create negative programs.

In her even, emotionless voice, Gay related the following information to a person sitting one evening in Sandy's living room:

> You were an informer for the Nazis. You were Jewish, wealthy, and comfortable; but you were a paid informer, and thus you now experience guilt for this.

As she wrote down the notes, Sandy thought, "Oh, brother! Are we going to get it now!" The person to whom Gay was speaking was Jewish in this life. Sheila came out of trance with a shocked look on her face. Sandy's hand was trembling. "How awful," she was thinking. As they turned to the man in the chair, he smiled looking much calmer than he had been when he came in. "That explains all those feelings," he said quietly. Both women breathed a sigh of relief. This was an early reading, and they had not yet learned to trust Gay. The phrase "That explains so much" was to become a frequent exclamation. Gay's presentation of material in her matter-of-fact manner and her sense of appropriate timing seldom caused any discomfort for the person to whom she was speaking. Sandy and Sheila had to learn to trust that this was so.

Not all persons receiving information did so with a smile and little emotion. Many people cried or wanted very much to cry. The two women began to realize, however, that this usually happened when Gay would tell people how beautiful, how talented, how sensitive, and how loving they were. Most people expect to hear bad things about themselves. They are all too ready to accept the worst; however, Gay's purpose is not to tell people what is wrong but what is right with them.

Her messages may contain negative or seemingly disastrous material, but this material is always accompanied with a "way out" — a perspective that offers freedom and personal power over one's own life. The following was a message to a frequent visitor of Gay's. The young man she was speaking to is a likeable, warm person who tries very hard to be spiritual but often struggles with what he feels to be bad or evil parts of himself:

> You are close to reaching new levels of understanding yourself. Use your higher self and guide to continue to aid you. The answers are within you but blocked much of the time by guilt. This guilt you feel makes you need to punish yourself and deny yourself unnecessarily. You do not have to cleanse yourself of anything in order to be spiritual. You are both spiritual and physical every moment of existence. You cannot get away from either spiritualism or materialism. By materialism here, I speak of enjoying the physical world and the earth itself. Much of your guilt comes from past existences. One in particular where you misused power and arranged many people's murders and their troubles in order to get further ahead yourself. You were involved in the beginning of the steel industry and very anxious to have many material goods. In other lives, as you know, you have been at the other extreme — almost to the point of ignoring physical existence. These two kinds of existences need balance. Once you were only concerned with physical gratifications — power, women, fortune. Others, only wished spiritual existence. You are here in this life now to learn balance. Also, things that you have done in the past, either in this life or previous lives, do not have to cause you to punish yourself.

Relief, understanding, and usually a feeling of calmness — these are the feelings reported by most people after talking to Gay. "She's comfortable and shows a concern for whomever she's talking to," one woman said after her third visit. "She's positive. She shows me what I can do rather than what I can't do."

During January of 1979, Sandy and Sheila were invited to speak to several classes taught by Jacob Schwartz, a well-known Philadelphia astrologer who teaches psychic phenomena at Temple University and adult education programs at local Y's. This was a new adventure for the two women, and they had no idea as to what they would do or how they would be received. The first class was an evening accredited class at Temple. There were about 25 people in the room. Most were not attuned to their work. They were college students taking a course for credit. Until now, they had spoken with groups who came to them for classes and seminars because of a mutual interest and an understanding of what they did. Jacob asked if Gay would talk to the class. Sheila gulped, as Sandy said, "Sure." A discussion as to format ensued. It was decided that the class members would submit questions on slips of paper with their first names only, and Gay would answer them. This seemed somewhat impossible to Sheila and Sandy, but they agreed to try. The questions were very similar to those asked in an individual session. "What kind of job should I look for?" "Should I go to Colorado with Henry?" "Should I continue with the medication I'm presently taking?" "What is the best environment for my spiritual growth?"

Sheila relaxed. Sandy concentrated on Gay's name and crossed her fingers. Gay began to talk. First she addressed the group, answering a general question about her relationship to Sheila. She said she was there "to enable you all to realize your own personal strength and power." She then spoke to each question as Sandy read them from the torn pieces of paper. To Sandy, to Jacob, and to the rest of the class, the answers seemed vague and general. However, at the end of the class individuals approached them to say: "That's exactly what I needed to hear"; or "She answered my question in a way that was very specific to me. Thank you."

This personal nature of the answers coming from Gay was something else that Sandy and Sheila had to learn about. Often it would sound vague or general to them, and then the person to whom Gay was speaking would say, "That's exactly what I was thinking this morning"; or "She describes my conflict perfectly. I know what she's saying." Here too, the two women eventually learned to trust and know that the words coming through were the right ones for the person hearing them.

The students in Jacob's class were curious as to what Sheila experiences during Gay's talks. This is a question frequently asked during readings. People would want to know if she was conscious of the material and able to remember what was said. Sheila is conscious as Gay speaks, but she usually does not know what the words will be before they are spoken. Often she will be having her own thoughts about the question or situation and find herself surprised by Gay's explanation. Occasionally she experiences feelings or images pertaining to the material being delivered, but most often she feels she is off to the side listening. When she comes out of trance, a sense of the material is in her conscious mind but will often fade rapidly, like a dream does if it is not reinforced by writing it down or repeating it aloud.

In December of 1977, Gay had spoken to Sandy and Sheila about the people who were coming to talk to her: "In what you call time and space, the information on those who need help is right there around them. It is close to their consciousness in this life."

Another time she said to a young man: "I can only see and sense from another perspective. In regards to life, only what you want to be known to me is known. This includes beliefs at the subconscious level you may not be aware of."

People hear what they are ready to hear. The material comes from their own consciousness. It is around them at the moment they are speaking to her. She feeds it back to them, often bringing it up to conscious levels of understanding, and always with a positive tone that will, hopefully, lead them to a better understanding of their own personal strength and power to create their own lives.

Chapter 5

Contacting Guides

ANN SAT LISTENING to Gay. This was her first reading, and she asked if she had a guide she could contact. Gay told her:

> You have a guide yourself. This guide's name is SERENA (spelled out) and was a friend in Atlantis, where you have been before. The contact has already been established, and she aids you especially in the choice of friends, and she can be reached through meditation. You can begin by relaxing your body and mentally, if not physically, surrounding yourself with trees. Trees give strength and good feelings to you, particularly evergreens or pine trees. The smell and feelings will be conducive to relaxing for you and trust that you are gaining wisdom. You may not get words at first, but ask for feelings of love and peace. They will be there for you. As you go about your day, flashes of amazing insight will happen. That is from your guide. Accept. Trust. Act on it. Friends important to you. Trust that she is helping guide you to loving people.

Six months later, Ann came for a second reading. She had questions about two new close friends about whom she felt especially good. She reported that, indeed, she had noticed frequent "flashes" or thoughts of insight coming to her. She then related the following experiences:

> I first felt my guide's presence one day while walking in the woods. The woods, you'll recall, is where Gay had told me I would be comfortable; and when I felt my guide, I knew what it was but I pulled away. Someone was with me, and I wanted my first contact with her to be special and when I was alone. Shortly after that, I awoke one night in the middle of an upsetting nightmare about a close friend. I was shaking and my body was covered with perspiration. I thought to myself that now was the time I needed to meet my guide. I had no idea what to expect, but I laid down and mentally created trees in my mind. The visualization was vivid, and I felt myself to be surrounded by trees. I calmed down. Then my guide came. She came as a voice that I could hear within my

head. She stated a message that gave me peace and then left immediately. There was no dialogue, and I felt that to be proper; although I guess I had thought that there would be, even though you [Sheila and Sandy] had not discussed with me the form of contact I could expect. Most important to me, however, was the feeling that this guide was not a separate person but very much a part of me – another part of myself that I had not known before. While she was talking, I knew she was me; and knowing that was very important to me. After she left, I fell into a deep, peaceful sleep.

Gay had begun telling Sheila and Sandy that she would be their guide from the beginning of their communications. Their attitude then was, "Okay. That's fun. Why not?" They did not take the idea too seriously. They did consistently question her about their lives during their weekly sessions. Neither woman thought much about having a "guide." At that time, they were much too taken with the idea of having past lives and a contact with the spiritual world. Right from the start, however, Gay insisted that everyone had guides. She gave each of Sandy's children the name of a personal guide to whom they could talk. Steven, who was nine years old at the time, had a boy-guide named Noman. Noman was a soul preferring spiritual life to physical life, and children to adults. Griffin, six at the time, could talk to a guide named Nevil, a female spirit who would visit him during sleep. The children thought this wonderful fun. Steven had always talked to imaginary playmates anyway, and this was one more. As the women began realizing the validity of the guide concept, they began to understand how real the child's world of invisible playmates could be. The Christian concept of guardian angels also took on new meaning. As they learned more about the new levels of reality to which they were being introduced, many old ideas they had viewed as silly or mythical were reevaluated. It was just a year or two before this time that Elizabeth Kubler-Ross had made a public statement that she, as a result of her work with the dying, had come to believe not only in life after death, but in guides; and, in fact, talked to hers daily. At the time, Sandy, who had read and admired her work, thought: "Oh brother! That brilliant woman has cracked. What a shame." Now, she silently apologized to Dr. Kubler-Ross.

When the readings began, Gay would tell people about their own guides. As with Ann, she would usually give them a name and a mental image – what she would call a "meditation" – to concentrate upon as they called for their personal guides. These meditations were often beautiful and poetic, and almost always called to the person's mind a scene or physical location where, at some time in his or her life, he/she had felt at peace. Sometimes she would refuse to give a name, and then tell the person that he or she would discover the name by simply relaxing and trusting his or her own mind. Guides' names were sometimes beautiful and exotic – names like Serena, Acrea, Deeana, Laureen; sometimes Biblical – like Daniel or Samuel; sometimes quite common – George, Philip, Ben, Diana, or even Hector. Gay would often spell the names, especially when they were supposed to be Greek, Atlantean or of some strange origin.

One instance involving the spelling of a guide's name happened during one of the first readings; and in addition to making everyone laugh, it caused Sandy to consider Gay's mental abilities. Gay was talking to a woman that she insisted she, Gay, knew in a past life. She began talking about a cousin named John, whom she insisted the woman should know.

Sandy: Why doesn't she know him?
Gay: She does.
Sandy: Why doesn't she recognize it?
Gay: (to the woman) You still have a fear of what is not seen.
Sandy: Is John a spirit?
Gay: Yes, Her guide. Spell it JON – take out the "h".

At no time during this exchange did Sandy spell the name John/Jon out loud. She was writing and speaking the name only. Gay had evidently "read" what she had written and corrected her assumed spelling of the name.

Gay would often give a person information on his or her past relationship to a guide. Often, as with Jon, there would be a past-life connection – a relative or friend. Sometimes these relationships were ancient, dating back to forgotten civilizations where perhaps the person enjoyed a lifetime of beauty and learning. Sometimes the relationship would be of a very practical nature – a man with musical ability being guided by a musician who had been a friend in a recent past life; or a man, now exploring psychic realms with out-of-body experiences, guided by two men with whom he had once explored the physical earth. At other times, however, the relationship of guide to person had never been manifested in a physical reality. These relationships begin on a spiritual plane. This is often true for people who prefer spiritual existence to physical existence, and so spend much time between lives. These people are often guides themselves when not incarnated. Gay is insistent upon the reality of a spiritual place of rest that she refers to as Arcadia. She will often tell people of their periods of rest and play in Arcadia and of relationships they develop there which often aid them while in physical focus. Perhaps there was a time when the Gods and humans did easily move between a spiritual reality and our physical reality, giving possible validity to our cultural myths. At the time Gay began talking about Arcadia, Sheila had never read Greek mythology and knew nothing of Arcadian nymphs and shepherds.

As is often the case when seemingly new ideas or concepts are finally accepted by the conscious mind, support for these ideas pours forth from the physical world. Sometimes unexplained experience finally fits the puzzle pieces into a whole — a finally closed gestalt. People began talking to Sandy and Sheila about "always" having felt a protective presence during their lives; or they would relate incidents of crucial experience — often involving danger to self or family — where suddenly they would hear a voice directing them, or intuitively know the right action to take to save the situation. Hearing these incidences became common occurrences as the women spoke to more and more people about their new perspective. An important part of Sandy's personal psychology fell into place with the concept of spiritual guidance, illustrating one of the possible ways in which our guides — our own higher aspects — lead us through patterns of growth and consciousness expansion.

In June of 1973, Sandy had decided to enter therapy for a second time. She was having difficulty in personal relationships and felt stuck in a destructive pattern which had repeated itself throughout her adult life. Most of the time, her main defense was to ignore any signals telling her that something was wrong with her life and to pretend that she had everything under control. But that avoidance became increasingly impossible as she finally faced her discomfort. Writing in her journal, after a lengthy discussion of the problems she had in her relationships, she finally admitted to herself that she had "voices" in her head:

> And then there's that "voice" in the back of my head, that intrudes into my thoughts at the least appropriate times and says "I love you." When fantasizing about a love situation, I could rationalize it; but it pops in when I'm thinking of work or the kids or just associating — pops in from nowhere, or somewhere deep and hidden — and my present consciousness of it is driving me batty. I can't call it up. If I'm thinking about it, it doesn't happen; but now, when it intrudes upon my thought process, I notice it —

something I previously would dismiss or rationalize. It's not a "front" thought, but feels as if it rises from the back and clamps down on the front of my brain, becoming louder than the other thoughts in my head. I can't continue without doing something in response to the voice. I must also deal with myself for my kids' sake. I don't want them suffering like this because of me.

A voice telling her "I love you" was driving her batty and causing her suffering. She felt the voice as a threat, as something terribly wrong with her, over which she had no control. In therapy she learned to let go of that desperate need for control, and the voice subsided — returning only occasionally. When it did, Sandy could accept it without feeling threatened. She "fit" the voice into a psychological model of reality. Her own subconscious rose up to make her aware of her repressed need for love. This was fine. It fit, and she was comfortable with the explanation; except that now the voice came when she was feeling loved. She would search around for a "deficiency" in her life, in her relationships. If a current problem could not explain the recurrence of the voice, she became uncomfortable with the psychological explanation. This was a minor irritation for the most part, however, and she was comfortable enough to even occasionally talk to other people about her "old" self and her "voice."

Then, in April of 1978, Sandy had another experience which satisfactorily completed her puzzle. She attended a four-day seminar given by Robert Monroe's Institute of Applied Science in Richmond, Virginia to experience Monroe's out-of-body training program. The excellently planned, step-by-step program moved its participants from normal consciousness through light states of trance or hypnosis to an expanded consciousness Monroe calls "Focus 12," which Sandy had already experienced many times as a "higher self" hypnosis. The four days were more important for her in terms of her emotional experience and acceptance by others, than by her learning new techniques for reaching altered states of consciousness. The climax came on Sunday morning, during the last sessions. Sandy wrote the following description of her experience in her journal:

> The material and sequence of the program did not offer much new to me. Focus 10 and Focus 12 (progressively deeper states of trance) were common enough states of consciousness for me because of my daily meditations — especially the morning one, when I'm awake and creative. The out-of-body part was good preparation for doing it at home...I had many of the same kind of experiences I have at home and not even as vivid and dramatic as

I'm used to; by Sunday, however, something happened that was very real and quite unexpected: an exchange of feelings with the various "parts" or "areas" of my inner self. Sunday morning I was very emotional and close to tears. During the last tape, my expanded being (my higher self) shouted at me from every corner or point of its being (it's as if I must interpret it spatially—an "out there" — kind of large, dark, rounded space or room with the words coming from every part and converging on me), "we love you." These are, of course, my old "voices" — those voices that have been in my head for years, trying to make me pay attention; and over the years, I eventually have—moving from a fear of them a few years ago, to yesterday morning's overwhelming emotional realization and acceptance that they spoke the truth — that (my higher aspects) do love me, and that I can love myself and others and it's okay. I don't have to be afraid anymore. These are lessons I've been learning for quite a while. They seem to have to be repeated over and over and over — on that emotional level, anyway!

Later, thinking over this experience of her "voices" and discussing it with Sheila, Sandy began to realize that she, too, had been guided during her life toward growth and expanded awareness. It mattered little that she had once explained the phenomena as her subconscious dealing with repressed needs: a psychological model was necessary and relevant during that period of her life. Now it was time to recognize a greater reality that included loving parts of herself—the parts of herself that were her Gay Bonner — and who gently prod her "normal," accepted consciousness toward greater understanding of who she is.

Sandy knows when she is communicating with Gay, whether that communication is directly through the mechanism of Sheila's body, or as words coming through her pen or typewriter, or as thoughts that "pop" into her mind giving her direction, answers, or reassurance. This knowing came out of a growing trust in the complex potentials of her own mind. The personification of guides; i.e., Gay Bonner, who calls herself a "thought form created by the energies of the people I talk to, as well as my own," simply makes the process easier. For some, this is limiting, and a concept of "higher self" or "higher energies" is a more acceptable form of description. David Spangler, the young mystic who at one time co-directed the community at Findhorn, Scotland, described his first meetings with a guide, John, in his book, *Revelation: The Birth of a New Age.* Later, David channeled beautiful material for an energy gestalt, or essence, he called

Limitless Love and Truth. Jane Roberts, who has a unique and wonderful relationship with an entity named Seth, struggles throughout her books to define who she is in relationship to him. Seth, whose communications have changed the lives of many people in the past ten years, describes himself as an "energy personality essence."[1] Trenna Sutphen channels for a "reincarnational self" named Athena.[2] David Paladin's "spooks" are people from the past with a helpful specialty as well as a philosophical turn of mind: the artist Kandinsky, a doctor named Gottlieb, and others.[3] Whatever the definition or form of presentation, the reality of these communications and value of these expanded states of awareness, in terms of personal growth, became obvious to Sandy and Sheila. They were also a lot of fun.

Sheila and Sandy have a close friend who has four guides. Al relates to them as if they are four distinct bullies who push him into various learning situations for his own good. One, Philip, is always complaining because Al does not listen. Maury wants him to pay more attention to his musical talent and comic aspects. Al, now a businessman with a large Philadelphia firm, was once a musician and stand-up comic. The other two are less active in Al's daily life. One called Star offers him spiritual experience and feelings of a "higher self".

Sheila has had some contact with various aspects of herself that are connected to Gay, yet somehow are further removed. One such personality presented herself briefly as Orca, a "bridge" personality to help her with the readings. On two occasions, Sheila spontaneously spoke for a personality whom Gay calls Nawa. This happened the first time one evening when Madeline and a male friend were there for a private session. Sheila's mood was easy, relaxed and open. Madeline's friend made an offhand comment about how much time he wasted in his life. Sheila, who had been sitting up, suddenly fell back on the couch (she later reported feeling gently pulled down) and began speaking in a distinctly different pattern than Sandy and Madeline had previously experienced. They knew this was not Gay Bonner. The words were simple and direct:

> You are never wasting time. Waste and time do not exist. Waste
> …nothing gets wasted. Everything changes. You can waste noth-
> ing. Every experience, every piece of material on earth only
> changes. You can have no waste. That is quite an interesting

---

[1] Roberts, Jane, *The Unknown Reality,* Vol. 2, p. 1.
[2] Sutphen, Dick, *Past Lives, Future Loves,* p. 38.
[3] Weisman, Alan, *We Immortals,* p. 199.

word. Then again, there is no time. Experiences are all, and since
there is neither waste nor time they do not exist. You can learn
from an experience, and in the next it changes. That is all. Maybe
you can think on it for a while... I only want to comment on your
words....The two words were quite interesting: waste and time.
All experiences are just to learn. Look at what you need also.

Sandy was struck, not so much by the content of the words, but
by the texture of the communication. This personality felt far removed
from the emotional tone of their physical reality. Gay was somewhat
removed from this reality, but Sandy could feel warmth and emotional
involvement from her. With this new personality, however, she could
feel no emotional quality in the communication. The voice was pat-
terned in a high, distinct lilting cadence, with no variance in the pattern throughout the entire speech; but, most of all, Sandy felt a vast
distance from the personality, as if it were – if space were applicable –
hundreds of miles away. They, of course, asked Gay what it was all
about and received the following explanation:

Gay: This other part of me had been in waiting for this night to
show itself. There may be more some other time.

Sandy: How does it work?

Gay: It is another frequency, and she (Sheila) must be more
relaxed.

Sandy: A higher frequency?

Gay: Yes, which she traveled to. She must go to our frequency
for the switch to take place.

Sandy: A further removed place?

Gay: Further away, but she traveled there.

Sandy: Why did she go down suddenly?

Gay: Because she was open to the pull. It was almost as a
magnet works. I said last week that she is close to another state of
consciousness change, and it was helped tonight. (11-29-77)

The second time Nawa spoke had to do with some possible
psychic work Sheila may be doing in the future. She has been very
intrigued with the possible physical explanations for what happens
during the exchange, when her normal consciousness switches off, or
over, and Gay begins to speak using her body. One night she experienced a very intense dream where she was given a physics formula that
would explain such frequency switches and possibly may explain her
interaction with Gay. In the dream, she felt: "I've got it! I know and
understand!" When she woke up, however, she could not remember

the specifics and was very disappointed. Realizing this was probably due to her doubts about her own conscious knowledge of physics, she and Sandy decided to have a session with Gay to learn more about the experience. Once again Nawa came through. And again, it was not so much the meaning of the words that was significant to the women, but the strangeness of the communication. She attempted to explain to them the physics principles behind frequency switching, but they were not ready to explore that area of learning in depth. It still awaits them. Gay told them that eventually they would meet a physicist who could help interpret the information for their intellectual understanding. At this point it was the experience of the communication and its potential for exploration that was most important to Sheila and Sandy.

Specific guidance for creative work was not a new idea to the women. Earlier, Sandy had encountered a similar, if less dramatic, experience, with a personal guide who called himself Easher. He had spoken a couple of words through Sheila during a private session, saying he was going to help Sandy with her writing. During a meditation on August 5, 1977, Sandy was questioning her creative abilities when, in a spontaneous vision, she met and conversed with a colorful character who claimed to be Easher. Mentally she was in a cabin that she had created for the purpose of communication with Gay. She wrote the following account immediately after it happened:

> I just went down into my cabin. I kept getting lost with many images and scenes that I wasn't retaining, so I very deliberately pulled myself into the cabin, put Gay in the chair, faced her, and asked for help on the book. After some discussion, I asked her about this Easher, who'd announced himself recently, and was told that he was an English minstrel, playwright, and tract writer from just before Shakespeare's time. He was, according to Gay, a reincarnational ancestor of mine.

At this point Sandy experienced Gay leaving; and suddenly a very buoyant, boisterous, young man began bouncing around the cabin, playing a mandolin and singing. She wrote:

> He said he has a lighter nature than I and was able to see the humorous side of life easier. He was, he declared, in touch with how we create our dilemmas and so was much more able than I to enjoy the scenes we create in our lives from a detached point-of-view. He does not falsely sympathize with stuck people but can see clearly that they make their own choices. In his physical life, he died at age thirty-one in a tavern brawl over a woman (or was it a boy? he laughed). I liked him, and he made me feel very good.

He gave her some practical advice about not seeing her writing as a struggle. When he left, he flew up through the chimney of the cabin, saying he enjoyed doing such things. Sandy came out of the trance a little flabbergasted. She usually did take life too seriously and was inclined to struggle with work she very much wanted to enjoy. Easher was to become part of her creative work as one of her guiding aspects.

Early in 1978, Sheila began holding ESP classes. The original format was directed toward the development of psychic abilities. Sheila used hypnosis as a tool for relaxing the class participants, teaching them to explore the altered states of consciousness most conducive to allowing the emergence of what she believed were everyone's innate psychic abilities. Each class explored some psychic ability – such as telepathy, clairvoyance, mind projection, psychometry, or the like – as well as undergoing a guided hypnosis that gradually took the class participants to a higher self or superconscious level of awareness. In this state of consciousness, they experienced expansive feelings, sometimes visions and dreams that were often precognitive or clairvoyant, and a sense of confidence. They found that they did indeed have these "weird" abilities; and many who had come out of curiosity, firm in the belief that they were not psychic, were surprised to find out otherwise.

One of the exercises Sheila did in these early classes had the class participants concentrate on items spread over a tray for a timed period. She would then cover the items and ask everyone to write down as many of them as they could remember. She usually did this experiment the first night of a new class, as it was designed to improve the concentration and increase the confidence of the participants. In one such instance, one of the students, Peggy, had said she did not know why she had come, as she was convinced that she was not psychic. She was curious, however, so she tried the experiment. The items on the tray were simple things Sheila had brought from home: a key, a button, a ring, and so on. After everyone had written their list, Sheila removed the cover so they could check their accuracy. Peggy began laughing, saying, "Wouldn't you believe it? I wrote something here that wasn't even on the tray. A nail file." Sheila did a double-take. She knew she had brought a nail file with the other things, but it was not on the tray. She checked the bag in which she had carried the items from home. The nail file was still in the bottom of the bag. She had missed putting it on the tray before the experiment. The class never again let Peggy say she wasn't psychic.

As the classes continued, one night in particular was assigned for interested advanced students. The class participants experimented with a great variety of experience. Sometime toward late summer of 1978, Sheila reevaluated the purpose of this class and then of all her classes. More and more people were making contact with their own guides. Many who had had sessions with Gay would call for advice or feedback on experiences they had that resulted from suggested meditations she had given them. The class participants were also asking if Gay could comment during the class on psychic events, giving them help and feedback where they might feel blocked. Sheila decided to change the emphasis of the classes from experimenting with ESP to contacting guides.

Again, using higher-self hypnosis and guided fantasies, she led the classes in an exploration of a guide contact. At the beginning of a new class series, she would lead the participants to an inner realm where they could meet their guides and, with trust, often receive names for those guides. Many had names from Gay, but those who did not usually "got" one in this altered state of consciousness. After the hypnosis session, people would discuss their experiences, giving one another encouragement and feedback. Then, through Sheila, Gay would speak to the group, answering any questions they had concerning the contacting of their guides, or experiences relating to possible communications from guides.

Almost everyone in the class experienced something during the hypnosis — from feelings of love to specific messages in the form of words, thoughts, or visions. Sometimes the contact did not occur in the formal setting of class but later at home, in dreams or meditations. As the weeks went by, people would relate their outside experiences with these communications to the class for feedback and support. Sometimes physical happenings in a person's life turned out to be messages from this guiding part of themselves — even words spoken to them by other people in their lives. They learned to be aware and open to any form of communication that may be offered them.

Many people developed abilities in automatic writing. Others could speak in trance for their guides. Most learned to trust their own thoughts and intuition, distinguishing between the usual clitter-clatter of their minds and the deeper knowing arising from their guide parts.

"Trust yourselves." The message Gay had been giving Sandy and Sheila for the past two years became a dominant theme in her messages to the classes. On August 23, 1978, in answer to questions from the class such as "Is my guide really David?" "What happened to me tonight?" "Was the message that popped into my head a message from Zachary?" she said the following before answering each specific individual:

> You all received, but sometimes you do not wish to know that you are recieving as you still believe you are not worthy of this; and I wish to tell you that everything is mind and that trust is more important. You have created us just as you create your physical friends; and we, in a sense, have created you and wish to help and send love. This is a feeling of love, and it means much to have it accepted. When you offer friendship and love to a physical person, it feels bad to have it not accepted; and this is the same, but your guides are also you, and you hurt yourself by refusing love.

Trust your own creativity. Believe in your own worth. These ideas are repeated over and over in the class transcripts. People in the classes learned to do this, and with the week-to-week reinforcement from one another and feedback from Gay, they began making meaningful contacts that had practical application in their lives, as well as expanded awareness of their total self.

Gay always stressed the idea that our guides are also part of ourselves:

> It is all your mind and your creation, as is your entire life and your physical friends. You help even to create each other, and your guides are your mind and a part of a greater you. You all have contact with your guides any time you wish, if you trust and ask for more. (8/22/78)

> Your guides are close to you all, as close as a change in frequencies or consciousness, and all send you love. (8/23/78)

> Understand that your guides are a part of you. Many of the everyday thoughts you have are now coming from this higher self. You often live in this consciousness, and you are not aware that you are already there. You are in constant communication, but unaware. Look around you and know that your life is the answer, as it unfolds. (9/12/78)

And so on. The ideas she stressed in regard to her relationship to Sheila and Sandy, she also gave to classes. She soon began emphasizing where development of the guide relationship could take the individuals in the class:

> Groups and classes such as this are necessary for a while until you can all learn that it is possible to live totally in the higher self. And

you will be your guide, and as a whole entity, there will be no doubt that you will live this communication. This is part of this new age. Until then, classes like this will enable you to learn to switch frequency. It is done now in a structured and forced manner, but this is how to learn. Feel yourself now. You all here have taken leaps in consciousness since I first spoke to each of you individually. This will continue, and you will know your answers in every minute of your existence. Every word spoken to you, every event, every person is a communication from your higher self. More groups like this one are meeting all over and are a good step. Contact with other realities need not be mysterious or frightening. I am possible because of you. You all create and help maintain my existence, and your own guides. Continue with this work, but keep in mind that contacts will come not necessarily through structure. Good night. (9/6/78)

Moving into new levels of consciousness. Becoming aware of who you are at any given moment. Becoming your guide. The class members were learning to trust themselves.

Sheila's Wednesday-night class continued for about seven months; and during that time, the class experimented with many new levels of consciousness and awareness. One of the most satisfying experiments was the development of a group or class spirit. Using guided meditation, the group learned to open themselves to one another in a manner which combined their collective energies to create what Sheila strongly felt was a group guide, or spirit. The members of the class, trusting their feelings and impressions, were able to express the communication of this spirit. When they first began feeling the connectedness with this entity, Gay confirmed their perceptions:

There is indeed a group entity, or spirit, if you wish to call it that. It is really the total consciousness forming a thought form very much like individual guides, but much stronger than each individual.

At a later session, using a light trance, the class members opened a communication with this spirit. A sensitive class member spoke for the group spirit:

I am George. George is my name. My name has many connotations: light, forever loving, beauty. Deep down inside we are all one. This is true what I say. We are one. We are all here tonight to help one another to become one with the universe.

Another woman described her experience during the communication:

> I saw a halo of light with rays streaming down to each one of us, sending energy back and forth. The light was carrying healing energy for our whole being—body, mind, and soul—uniting us all as one and part of a larger whole.

A man reported:

> I saw a wave of energy to my right. Before George spoke, I could see a vast universe....

The group spirit spoke through various class members, telling each individual of a higher creative and psychic potential. The class had reached a new level or form of guide communication, which gave them many beautiful and close feelings of positive energy and shared love.

Not all guide communication is so serious and ponderous. In fact, a good part of the time Sandy and Sheila found their "messages" to be playful and fun. Gay frequently exhorts them to "not be so hard on themselves."

Sandy was going through one of her self-deprecation periods in May of 1979. As she felt self-doubt so she created evidence in her life to support these feelings. She was often aware of the silliness behind this behavior, but also allowed herself to become caught in it despite the awareness. This was one such time. Her feelings of doubt centered on the issue of balance. She was seeing herself as too much of this and too little of that—in whatever qualities were the concern of the day. She happened to buy a book on color healing. In that book was a test on how to determine, using the letters in one's name, the colors predominant in one's personality with, of course, corresponding character traits. Now, Sandy knew better than to do this. These kinds of experiments never worked out the way she thought they should, and she always took them much too seriously; but she could not resist. Of course her colors were heavily unbalanced, and all of her friends were balanced—in harmony, at peace with themselves.

"It's just a silly, meaningless test," she argued with herself, all the time allowing its results to dampen her mood and reinforce her current feelings of self-doubt. That afternoon, as she lay on her bed in a light, restful trance, she experienced many of her usual feelings: vibrations in her body, movement around her, a lifting sensation, and so on. These sensations always gave her the feeling of being in touch with the parts of herself that were larger than her usual focus. Deciding that it was time to start dinner, she opened her eyes and began to sit up.

As she did, she saw above her a huge gold-beige colored spider (three-to-four inches in diameter) scurrying across the white ceiling.

"Good grief," she thought, "how am I going to get that out of the house?" and she fell back on the bed as the "spider" faded into the ceiling. But before she had time to think about that, she began to see, in front of her open eyes, a series of pulsating colors which would begin as intense blobs of color that would widen, then fade, then change. All of the colors she experienced were those missing from her "test." When she began to think, to hear her thoughts, she knew that the colors were coming from her own energy — her aura, and she began to laugh. "They" (her guides) had played a joke on her with the impossible spider in order that she not take herself so seriously.

One of Sheila's classes experienced a joke in the form of what would usually be called a "coincidence." The class was the last of a six-week scheduled meeting on Monday mornings at the Mind Matters office in Washington Crossing, Pennsylvania. There were several people lying on the floor with Sheila, eating a cake that one of the class members had brought for the occasion. Sheila was discussing the effects in our lives of negative unseen influences, stressing that awareness and positive thought were the tools we all have for lessening their effect. She had been telling a story about a seminar she and Sandy had attended on psychic matters. The leader had told the group that he was aware that FBI agents were spying on the activities of the seminar — without identifying themselves as such. This had potentially negative effects, and he wanted the participants to be aware of the situation. As Sheila told the story, one of the students asked if she and Sandy had ever experienced anything of that nature. As Sheila answered, "No, we feel very protected," the door of the office burst open and there, in full uniform, clipboard in hand, was a local policeman, looking as astonished and confused as the class was flabbergasted! He had entered the wrong office, and they helped him find what he thought he had been looking for. Later, when Gay spoke to the class, she had these comments on the event:

> The policeman had no other choice at the moment, for he was not conscious of being drawn in here. He "chose" to enter to illustrate a point. This *is* a class in psychic development, and this is just an illustration of thoughts and their power and your power. Just a little cosmic joke!

Awareness that all human beings are creators of their own universe, and that that universe is a rich and multilayered matrix extending far beyond usual conscious focus, leads one to a new valuing of personal experience and all that one can learn from that experience. Guides are a helpful part of tapping into the richness of that learning, whether they are communicating with deep spiritual feeling, helpful thought and insight, physical events or jokes. All are forms of creativity available to everyone.

Chapter 6

Discovering Beliefs:
HOW WE CREATE OUR REALITY

I

SANDY'S NEW TAPE RECORDER had broken. Aggravated, she asked Gay why:

Gay: Sometimes machines break, like people.

Sandy: But it's practically new!

Gay: Some people are not old, either. Treat it nice.

Sandy: What did I do wrong?

Gay: You are stuck in that thought. Stop for a minute and think what you said about "I thought I did something wrong." That is one of your beliefs. Always asking "what did I do wrong?" Give up that belief.

Sandy: Why do I believe that?

Gay: You always have believed it, or the opposite – trying to shows others where they are wrong.

Sandy: Yes. I know I swing from one to the other now. Where does it all stem from?

Gay: Where all beliefs stem from. It has no start.

Sandy: Good grief, Gay! It has to start somewhere! Where does all this garbage start?

Gay: You are a perfect experiment and need to start believing as you do so you can experience and learn. You only want to learn all there is.

Sandy: You mean we actually *give* ourselves these beliefs?

Gay: Yes, so you can play the game. You take a belief. In fact, you are only really pretending them. You know deep down that you are a perfect experiment.

Sandy: Whose experiment?

Gay: Your own; and you want to learn everything there is. They are your toys – these beliefs. You can look at them. You can break them apart. You can build them up or build them apart.

This conversation took place in September of 1977, and Sandy was extremely agitated throughout the session. She had always firmly believed in cause and effect. Cause and effect implies a starting point. Events begin and events end. Something brings them about, and something else ends them. Gay was again asking her to stretch her concepts about reality and jump out of her comfortable time-and-space focus. Later that year, during a reading with a close friend, the issue of cause and effect was brought up again. "Where," they asked, "do problems start?"

Gay: This is for all of you. You are solving the universal problems, and they just are. You are all unique and yet form the very same questions. It is the whole universe working with you to create one and the same back-to-the-knowing in the total center of X. You are all contributing to this higher consciousness by taking and solving the universal questions. (11/26/77)

That was all well and good. We are all perfect experiments solving universal problems; but what does all that mean as we plow through our daily lives with their emotional ups and downs, and their frequent, aggravating setbacks and occasional tragic standstills? Sandy and Sheila had heard the phrase "I create my own reality" several years earlier, while they were still in therapy. Someone had painted a poster with those words and hung it up on the group-room bulletin board. Sandy, seeing it for the first time, thought, "Yes, that's certainly true in a psychological sense." It was easy to see its truth from that perspective. She was in the process of learning how her perceptions of others and herself colored her relationships and interactions with the world. If she felt frightened and defensive and acted distant and hostile then the others around her would respond in kind—distant and hostile. Her behavior, and its inconsistent corollary to her real feelings, had created a lifetime of psychological mish-mash. Yes, it was true that she created her psychological reality. At the time, she gave no further thought to the poster. The words continued to creep into her consciousness, however; and as she and Sheila began their psychic journey, she would come to realize that they were much more literal than she had ever dreamed.

> Experience is the product of the mind, the spirit, conscious thoughts and feelings, and unconscious thoughts and feelings. These together form the reality that you know. You are hardly at the mercy of a reality, therefore, that exists apart from yourself or is thrust upon you. You are so intimately connected with the

physical events composing your life experience that often you cannot distinguish between the seemingly material occurrences and the thoughts, expectations and desires that gave them birth.[1]

Seth was telling his readers that their minds literally create their reality. Gay was saying the same thing. Sandy put this information aside, dismissing its concreteness and insisting on symbolic or psychological interpretation; until one day she was hit with a very expensive realization. She was still reading *The Nature of Personal Reality*. Seth was repeating his basic theme over and over. Driving to work on a beautiful October morning in 1976, a month or so after she and Sheila first met Gay, she felt a reluctance to work. She was selling pharmaceuticals; and her day consisted of driving from doctor's office to doctor's office, discussing her company's products. As she drove to her first call, she had a passing thought: "I just don't feel like working. Wouldn't it be nice to have just a little car accident?" She dismissed the thought and continued on with her work. About 1 PM, after leaving a drug store where she had made a call, she went to her car to pick up new materials before visiting a doctor whose office was just up the street from where she had parked. The street was normally very busy, but on this day, there was construction a block away, and the traffic had been detoured. She saw no cars coming in either direction as she opened the car door, leaned across the front seat, and searched for the materials she needed. This action took about twenty seconds. But just as she began to move back across the seat, she heard a crash. Her open door had been hit by another car which had evidently turned the nearby corner. Out of the car climbed a perplexed, elderly man, apologizing profusely for his misjudgment of distance. The street was still empty, and he should have had plenty of room to miss her completely. She was furious! The door was badly damaged, and although a policeman managed to shut it, it would not open again. Later, she realized that she had narrowly missed being hit herself. But, of course, that was not what she had "created"! Driving home, after calming down somewhat (she had learned that according to Pennsylvania law she was at fault, as the driver's door should never be opened into the traffic; and so the expense of the accident was hers), she suddenly remembered the thought she had had earlier in the day. "Oh, my goodness! I did it!" She had been blaming the old man's poor vision and slowed reflexes. After all, everyone opened the driver's door to get out of a car — no matter what the law said. But here it was. She was

---

[1] Jane Roberts, *The Nature of Personal Reality*, 1974, p. xviii.

confronted by her own thought and began to realize her own responsibility in drawing the event to herself. With a silent apology to the old man (and a curiosity as to his psychic part in the event), she had her first conscious lesson in how her reality is created.

Thoughts and feelings create reality. Reality does not create thoughts or feelings. It all seemed so upside down. The two women were, however, beginning to turn with the idea, to see the world from this new perspective. Many areas of their lives which had before seemed hopelessly out of control began to make sense.

Lurking behind our thoughts and feelings are all the beliefs we hold about ourselves and the world we live in. Those beliefs determine what we think and how we feel. If we believe that others are unkind and interested in only themselves, then the people we come in contact with will be unkind and interested only in themselves. Our reality will thus be confirmed. If we believe that people are basically good and helpful, then the people we meet will be good and helpful. If we believe the world is safe, we will experience safety. If we are fearful and expect to be hurt, then we will be hurt. We can, however, as Seth points out, become "so intimately connected with the physical events...that often one cannot distinguish between the seemingly material occurrences and the thoughts, expectations, and desires that gave them birth." The challenge for Sandy and Sheila, then, became one of discovering exactly what they believed about themselves and the world they lived in.

"Watch your conscious thoughts" was Seth's suggestion for getting in touch with beliefs. This sounded easy enough, but both Sandy and Sheila found it to be much harder than they thought it would be. We are so much a part of our own thought processes that we screen out the hypnotic clitter-clatter that passes through our mind constantly. Meditation and self-hypnosis had helped the two women become more aware of their own thoughts, but catching themselves in their basic beliefs was quite a challenge. They developed a feedback system between themselves in order to catch each other when either one presented beliefs as facts. "All men ultimately withhold their feelings," one or the other would say. (They both at different times, held this belief about the opposite sex.) "Hey, that's only a belief. Not a fact." Oops! Caught. And so this kind of exchange became a habit between them. Remembering that the "facts" of our experience are only our "beliefs" about reality brought the ideas or feelings under discussion into a new perspective — one in which the undesirable reality could be open to change. Beliefs are necessary in our world. They are what hold us together. They can, however, be changed; and then the world we are living in can become the world we consciously want to live in.

Our language is often a key to our basic beliefs and often reflects what we believe we deserve to have in the world. During Sheila and Sandy's second trip to Arizona, in October of 1977, they met a young man named Dan. Actually, Sandy met him first. Shortly after their arrival, she decided to go down to the swimming pool and enjoy the outdoor jacuzzi. She was sitting in the warm, swirling water when an attractive young man walked up and painfully lowered himself into the whirlpool. Sandy's maternal instinct rose to the surface as instantaneously as the bubbles in the water, and she sympathetically asked what was wrong. He had hurt his back and could hardly move, he complained. It happened often, and this time he did not even remember the cause. She learned that he, too, had come for Dick Sutphen's hypnosis training seminar. For the next few days, she hovered over him like a mother hen. She supplied him with pain pills from her company, talked a physician attending the seminar into writing a prescription for him, drove him to the drugstore, and offered him much consolation. Nothing helped. Finally she suggested that he talk to Gay. Sheila and she had told a few people at the seminar about Gay and the readings they had recently begun giving at home. One new friend had already spoken to Gay directly. Sandy assumed that Dan had heard them talking about it and knew what talking to Gay meant. He agreed that anything which might help his discomfort was desirable, so he followed Sandy and Sheila back to their room. Upon entering, Sheila immediately lay on the bed to put herself into trance. Sandy reached for her notebook and pen and sat on the opposite bed waiting for Gay to speak. Dan wandered around the room looking for a glass of water to take an aspirin when Gay's voice suddenly boomed:

> Often you use the phrase "get off my back." Now it is too many people on your back....Several people are on your back. You can only take so much pressure. You are important too. Believe that. Believe you need something too, and this may help you.

Dan jumped a foot. "I thought you were going to get some automatic writing or something!" After his initial shock was over, he acknowledged that he often uses the phrase "get off my back," and indeed believed that he had to take care of many other people's problems.

Watch what you think or say, to discover what you believe.

How often do we bandy about cliches, each of us choosing the appropriate one to reflect our beliefs and manifest our reality. "I feel as though the world is on my shoulders." That is a favorite of Sandy's, and she realized that her shoulders were the focal point for most of her bodily tension when she was under pressure. One young man who came for a reading was reminded by Gay that his mother often told him, when he was a child, that he "had ants in his pants." He believed it; and now, as an adult, he suffers from itching on the anterior of his anatomy — particularly when he is restless. How many people suffering from hemorrhoids say over and over, "That's a pain in the ass!"?

Sheila learned a painful lesson in how to discover beliefs during December of 1978. Mind Matters was slowly growing during those days, and Sheila had repeatedly said to Sandy, "When are we going to get a break?" or "I wonder if this is the break we've been waiting for?" She was dancing a jig at a Christmas party when she got her "break." She broke her foot and spent the next six weeks in a cast and on crutches. Right after it happened, she questioned Gay about why it had happened to her. "You asked for it." She did not understand, but Gay insisted. "You asked for it."

"How could I have asked for anything so dumb?" Sheila cried. Then it hit her. Of course. She had been asking for a break for several months, and here it was. The next step was to examine her thoughts to determine if she could see why the break was in her foot instead of with Mind Matters. She had to admit that she was ambivalent and unclear as to what she really wanted to happen with her business and new career; and that even below that ambivalence, she was unsure as to whether or not she deserved the success she thought she wanted. These hidden beliefs had blocked what she had consciously thought she was asking for. The intensity and concentration behind her request for a "break" were strong enough to manifest one — but not the one she thought she would get. As it turned out, her break did bring gifts of insight. Gay had repeatedly told her that there were no accidents. Breaking a foot while dancing an Irish jig at a party certainly seemed like an accident. She now had to admit that she had manifested this particular "accident," just as Sandy has manifested her car accident. During the next six weeks, Sheila also learned about being still and accepting help. Overall, the experience gave her much insight and learning.

Physical events in our lives are clues to our beliefs. The broken foot, the sprained back, the smashed car door — all are clues to the inner beliefs that create our reality. Always ask what can be learned after an event — even the positive events.

Sandy and Sheila had a friend visiting England who found herself wandering in the streets of London with no money and two days to wait before her plane was leaving. She met a strange, little man who took her to a family where she was cared for during those days and had a lot of fun as well. She learned that if she trusted and felt deserving, she would draw caring, loving people to her. It had been very important to her at the time to feel that she was deserving. Many of us do not feel that we deserve positive responses from others or positive events in our reality. It is often a deep feeling of unworthiness that prevents us from having the reality we think we believe we want.

Feelings are another clue to our beliefs. When we are in the midst of an event or among people, if we honestly watch our feeling responses, we can discover much about the creative material with which we manifest our reality.

Sandy discovered the answer to a large part of her most perplexing behavior during the first year she sold pharmaceuticals. She believed she wanted to be a loving, caring mother toward her two sons; however, whenever they were sick, her initial response to the situation would be anger. This had puzzled and pained her ever since her older son's birth. She always found that in order to properly care for them, she had to first step back from the situation and feel a surge of anger run uncontrollably through her body before her caring, maternal feelings could surface. She felt that she was a bad person — an unnatural mother. Then, during the first summer that she worked for the pharmaceutical firm, she became very ill with pleurisy which later developed into pneumonia. She had been sick very few times in her adult life. In fact, she could remember being sick as a child only one or two times, with conventional childhood diseases like measles. Since she was unaccustomed to being sick, she continued to work even though she felt terrible. This worsened her condition and finally drove her to the doctor, who told her she had a slight touch of penumonia and should be home in bed. She went home; but as she began to undress, an extreme and unaccountable fear came over her. The panic that she experienced was new to her and made her feel as if she were going to die. She was in therapy at the time and arranged to go to a group session that evening. The fear stayed with her. When she arrived at the session, her therapist looked at her white face, told her to lie on the mat and go into her feelings. She was terrified, but did as she was told. She felt herself falling into a blackness, into a terror she had not known existed. She had always prided herself on never feeling fear. It was as if she had long ago decided that to survive she must never be afraid. As she fell into the blackness, she moved far back in time until, unfolding in her mind's eye, was a long-forgotten event. She was one or two years old. She could see the trailer where she lived with her young, inexperienced parents. She was crying in her crib, and her face was red with fever. She had known that she had scarlet fever around that age but had not remembered the event. Standing over her was her young, frustrated, anxious mother, her face contorted with rage. She just did not know what to do and responded to the sick child with anger. Sandy saw her father pull her mother away. She re-experienced all the fear that her mother's rage had invoked. She had learned then that it was bad to be sick. If she became sick, then she did not deserve to live. Others had a right to be angry with her. She had internalized her mother's anger as right and just, and now she reacted in kind to her own sons in spite of her rational desire to behave otherwise. As an adult, anger replaced fear in similar situations. The pneumonia had come at a time in her life when she was ready to face the extreme limits of these repressed feelings. She had a supportive environment in which to explore the roots of her terror. Following her feelings as she had, she learned of several beliefs she held about herself and her environment — beliefs that had been controlling her emotions and behavior. She also learned to sympathize with her mother, who she could see for the first time as a very young, frightened nineteen-year-old girl, with the over-whelming responsibility of a sick baby. She let go of many negative and controlling beliefs that evening.

Following your feelings need not be so dramatic. Most of us can simply watch our emotional barometers and learn about our beliefs. The people we draw to us in our lives often mirror our own concepts, and becoming conscious of our responses to their behavior will often lead us to more self-awareness. "He makes me so angry when he behaves like a child!" "She never takes responsibility for anything, and it makes me angry!" "I feel very frightened when my friends begin acting silly." How many of us were never allowed to be children? to not be responsible? to be silly?

Gay is often a source of information for people concerning their hidden beliefs. All of the readings deal to some extent with beliefs. Most often people will say, "Oh, yeah! That's true. I just didn't realize that I believe that." One young man asked several questions about childhood friends whom he felt did not like him. Gay talked to him about some of his very personal and deeply hidden beliefs:

> There are some personal beliefs that you need to examine and realize that these beliefs are not true in every reality. In the reality you have created, they appear to be true; but as you realize they structure only your own reality, you can move into acceptance and love. You assume that there are those whose lives are problem-free, and that they are in a sense happy and perfect. You then compare yourself to this idea in your mind. The friends you think of have many problems of their own. (9/79)

He had problems. It appeared to him that his friends did not, and that they, therefore, were better than he was and would not like him. His behavior toward them brought about a response that reinforced his beliefs. It was now time for a change.

Sheila will sometimes experience physical discomfort while going into trance to do a reading for someone. Often those physical symptoms reflect actual physical problems of the person, or some kind of psychological corollary. One summer day, the symptoms that appeared reflected a hidden belief of a young woman about to talk to Gay. The windows in Sandy's living room were open, as it was a warm, sunny day. The three women could hear the whirr of a lawnmower cutting grass in a field across the way. As Sheila lay down to go into trance, she began to experience congested sinuses, itching eyes, and a scratchy throat — all the signs of allergy — but she did not have any allergies. The symptoms were so severe that Sheila could not relax enough to allow Gay to come through. She sat up in frustration. Joy, the woman having the reading, looked at her and remarked: "It's problably because of the cut grass. Boy! If I hadn't had my shots this week, I'd probably be as miserable as you look right now."

Sheila thought, "Oh, that's it." She lay back, the symptoms abated, and Gay came through with the following for Joy:

> The allergy symptoms were yours, and I do want to comment on this as they will lessen if you begin to see yourself as free from being attacked. You have fears from these two past lives, as though you will be attacked because you felt you were a bad person. Even grasses, trees, and particles in the air have consciousness and will do these kinds of functions for you, such as attacking you. When you can be rid of this fear, the allergies will lessen. In the meantime, you are wise to protect yourself. Also send love out into the air, and it will help lessen these attacks. All leading back

to your fears of retaliation from these lives. Lately, however, I do
see a great break away from all old beliefs, but guilt still heavy
here....

Joy seriously considered what Gay had to say and began to
examine her thoughts, behavior, and feelings for beliefs about deserving to be attacked. She reported later, after having taken positive
action to overcome her fear of attack, that her allergies had lessened
considerably, and that she was able to discontinue her medicine.

Sandy had a similar physical problem with which Gay was able
to help her. For years, she had recurring sore throats. They were never
serious enough to make her really sick but would cause her discomfort
and annoyance. She asked Gay about them. "Change your thoughts
and see yourself saying whatever you wish with no fear of reprisal
from anyone." Sandy realized that she had always believed she talked
too much, or that she often said the wrong thing. She began to watch
when the sore throats occurred. Soon she was able to see that they
usually happened after some incident in which she believed she talked
too much, or revealed too much of herself to people she did not trust,
or said something she feared was unacceptable to someone else. As she
discovered these connections, the sore throats lessened.

We all have a Gay within us — a higher self or our own guides;
and as we learn to listen for messages from these areas of our mind, we
can use this knowledge to discover beliefs. One of the earliest experiences that Sandy had with her higher self involved a struggle she had
had for years. She thought she was fat. Her rational mind would tell
her that she was crazy, but a very deep part of her was convinced that
she was fat. And, indeed, she would begin to "feel" fat. Soon she
would gain five pounds; so she was always dieting and complaining
about being fat. Then she bought a self-hynposis tape designed for
people who needed to lose weight so she could work on her fat. The
procedure involved going deeply into trance; visualizing yourself in an
internal drama, thin and attractive, with your friends exclaiming how
terrific you look; some very strong affirmations about eating what,
and only as much as is good for you; and a trip to the superconscious,
or higher self, to determine the source of the problem. A conditioned
subject by now, Sandy sat in her orange living-room chair going deeply
into hypnotic trance, as the soothing and authoritative voice spoke
through her cassette recorder. She easily moved into a "higher" state
of consciousness, where she could communicate directly with her own
guides. Once there, at the recorded suggestion, she asked the big ques-

tion: "Why am I fat?" As soon as the words left her mind, a loud, inner voice, coming from the back of her head, screamed into her mind, "YOU ARE NOT FAT. YOU JUST LIKE TO STRUGGLE!" She came out of the trance dumbfounded. As she thought about it, she had to admit that she was not fat. It was always simply a question of adding and subtracting five pounds to her weight on a regular and frequent basis. She began watching the pattern and soon realized that she added the weight at times when her life was running the smoothest. During times of emotional turmoil or upheaval, she would drop the weight without giving it a thought. She did believe that she had to be engaged in a struggle of some kind and weight had given her a convenient tool for this end.

During the spring of 1978, Sheila and Sandy found that they had to face some of their beliefs which neither of them had ever thought about before. Money. They began to be confronted with people and events which increasingly brought to the surface uncomfortable feelings about making money, having money, spending money, asking for money for their services, and handling the money that was beginning to come into Mind Matters. But they began to realize that if they were going to be able to do the psychic work they were beginning to love, they would have to have money in order to live. They were, by this time, seeing that the work they were doing with people was valuable and deserved a chance to be developed further. But how? They needed money, and it seemed as though most of their energy and time was going into jobs that had only the purpose of bringing in money. Could they earn a living doing what they wanted to do? Or could they somehow have enough money to do what they wanted without expending time and energy working where they did not want to be? All of this was coming to conscious awareness, when they met a man from Philadelphia whose main purpose in this life was to make money. He became a regular weekly client for about seven months, during which time he would talk to Gay about his financial dealings. It was then that Sheila and Sandy found that they had many hidden beliefs about the nature of money and their relationship to it. They decided to explore their subconscious on the subject. Never during all the years of therapy, and in the year and a half they had worked with Gay, had they ever thought to ask about money. When they hypnotized each other, they found some startling results. They took turns putting each other into deep trance then moved their consciousness up and out into a superconscious or higher-self state where they discovered what they believed about money.

Sheila counted Sandy up into her higher self. Sandy experienced the beautiful floating feeling she associated with this state, feeling lighter and lighter as she expanded outward into a realm of light and beauty. Before Sheila reached the usual count of eight, Sandy began to see the clear image of a Baptist church that had been in the neighborhood where she grew up in Miami, Florida. She thought that very strange, as she had never attended the church and, in fact, had been afraid of the zeal and religious fervor of the people she knew who did go there. She had attended the more sedate Lutheran church in her neighborhood to avoid the constant pressure of the zealous Baptists. They were always recruiting young people and had frequently made her uncomfortable with their implicit threats of hell and damnation because she was not one of them. Then, as she lay there watching the image of the church, suddenly all kinds of thoughts crowded into her mind. "Money is the root of all evil." "People who have money are greedy or evil or selfish or whatever." "It's harder for a rich man to get through the eye of a needle..." "Spiritual people are poor." "To be spiritual, one must struggle with the material aspect of life." "Suffering is good for the soul."

All sorts of religious cliches came to the surface. Thoughts and ideas that she had never consciously known were a part of her floated up and swirled around the Baptist church. She had assumed that she had long ago left these ideas behind, that she had become too sophisticated for such clap-trap! But there it was. She did believe money was bad and usually chose not to think about it at all. Consequently, she had struggled most of her adult life with having just enough money to live comfortably. She had managed, but never with ease.

Next it was Sheila's turn. As she moved into her higher self, she had many fears. Sheila experiences her communications through feelings and words that pop into her mind. Now she felt a lot of fear. She let herself sink into it and soon began to receive thoughts about its nature. Her deepest belief about money was rooted in many past lives where repeatedly she had something that was taken away. If she were to allow herself to have enough money to be comfortable—to have the material things that she wanted in her life—then as soon as she thought she had had it, something or someone would come and take it away. She had found it easier to do without than to constantly feel the threat of loss.

Sheila and Sandy now knew their beliefs about money. The next step was to do something about them. The most important step had been taken; often just recognizing a limiting belief as a belief and not as a fact is enough to bring about change. Once we become consciously aware of the hidden or blocking belief, we can, simply by watching our thoughts, let go of the belief, lessening its influence on our lives. Sandy found this relatively easy to do with the weight problem. Money was another matter, however, but both women knew that they would benefit by taking active measures to counter the limiting beliefs they had discovered they had about money. The first step was to suspend their disbelief that a change in their reality could occur. Sheila had to allow that it was possible to give something to herself without it being taken away. That is, she had to suspend her disbelief that she was worthy of having what she wanted in her life. Sandy had to accept the idea that people who had money were no more or less spiritual than people without money, and that she could have as much money as she needed to live a comfortable life and still be a good person. They knew that they could not simply say, "Well, I will now begin to believe that I am deserving of having lots of money and be spiritual, too." They did not believe that. They could, however, mentally suspend their disbelief.

The next step was to introduce new beliefs to their subconscious. Both women were now practicing self-hypnosis daily, so they designed a new program. First they visualized themselves having as much money as they needed to do all the things they wanted. Sandy saw herself at home each day, sitting at her typewriter, doing the writing she wanted to have the time to do. Sitting next to her typewriter was a bank book with enough money in it to comfortably care for her family for at least two years. Sheila saw herself doing readings and holding classes, with no concern for money, as she too had plenty in the bank. They then decided also to allow themselves a little fun, so they visualized themselves skiing in Austria the next winter. The idea is to create as many visual images as possible of what you want and then feed these images, these dramas, into the subconscious during the profoundly relaxed state of hypnosis. The subconscious, receiving this concentrated programming, will begin to believe in the new reality. The old reality of limited money and struggle with the material aspect of life will then lose its potency and die.

The last step was to design new verbal affirmations to counteract the old, limiting beliefs. An affirmation should always be stated as a positive. For instance, Sandy could not say to herself, "Money is not evil," or even, "Spiritual people are not always poor." She knew that the subconscious tends to ignore "not" and pick up key words—in this case "evil" and "poor," which would only reinforce her negative core beliefs. Her affirmation was then stated as "Money is a positive force in my life." Sheila's read, "I deserve to always have as much money as I want" and "I keep what I have for as long as I want to."

This procedure can be used for any area of life. Discover the limiting beliefs. Suspend your disbelief about changing your reality. Visualize the way you wish your reality to be. Counteract the old belief with new, positive affirmations. In Chapter 12 of this book, specific techniques for attaining the best state of consciousness to accomplish these goals are outlined. Methods can help. There are many, however, and they are not necessary. Self awareness and a willingness to confront the feelings that self awareness may bring to the surface is the only "method" necessary.

Sandy and Sheila often discovered, as they did with money, that they had similar or interlocking beliefs that blocked their business progress or their personal growth. One such area became evident during the summer of 1979 and illustrates the process of discovering beliefs and following through to effect positive change. They had met a young woman who ran a secretarial service and wanted to exchange some of her services for Mind Matters events. To save valuable time, Sheila decided to accept her offer and arranged for her to do a mailing of the periodic Mind Matters newsletter.

She did a beautiful job in record time. The newsletter was artfully laid out and typed perfectly — except that Sheila's phone number was incorrect in both places where typed on the page. Sheila had recently moved and this was the first time her new phone number had been mailed to the Mind Matters mailing list of some three hundred people. Most of the appointments for Mind Matters were made on her phone. She was very angry and upset and spent the next two and a half days writing postcards to the entire mailing list with the corrected number. She was feeling very strongly that "No one else did anything right." "I can't trust anyone to do anything for me." And so on. One astute friend of hers recommended that she ask the woman who had made the mistake to send out the cards. "What? Are you crazy? I just *know* she'd botch it! I can't trust her."

"You don't trust anyone to help you," he countered. She stopped and stared at him. It was true. She didn't. She had a flood of memories of others goofing just one or two details of anything she and Sandy had given them to do. Something always went wrong — a detail incorrect, like the phone number, or the job or assignment never completed for some reason or another. Sheila realized a pattern — a pattern of drawing to her people who either made mistakes or did not complete their work; or drawing mistakes out of people who usually did competent work. She realized that she only trusted Sandy, and the two of them insisted on doing all the details of their business themselves.

She discussed this with Sandy, who, seeing the truth of the insight, remembered her own overwhelming feelings of relief after the first seminar they conducted together. That seminar had been the first time in her life that she had worked closely with anyone in a creative endeavor who she felt held up his or her end, without feeling as if she had to do everything herself. Since that point, she had trusted Sheila; but now, she realized, she trusted no one else.

They could see the pattern — the physical manifestations of deeply ingrained beliefs of which they had not become conscious until this latest event. To delve into the beliefs underlying the physical reality, they talked, mirroring back to each other the words they were saying. "No one ever does anything right." "I always have to do everything myself." "To be helped admits a weakness in me." "I don't deserve to be helped." "Other people really don't want to give me anything." These deep beliefs that they suddenly could see were in their way if they wanted to expand their psychic work and reach more people. They asked Gay about it, and she confirmed their findings:

> You already have the beliefs that are involved here. They are easily brought now to conscious awareness through discussion. It was important for you to see this pattern and this is preventing your growth both in business and spirituality. A need here to let go and trust. Accept help. Realize this work is not just yours, but to share. Not that you need to sacrifice individuality to a group, but to see that the burden is not all yours. That both the work and joy can be shared. You give energy and you give love and joy but insist on doing everything yourselves. This is not the new age laws. These 'laws' insist on return of energy, and by not accepting this you block your own efforts in the physical world. There needs to be some energy put into your work by others, so that you can be energized to give even more. I am not suggesting a large group or organizations — just acceptance of energy that can be given you by others. There are those who can, but you must believe this. Again, it is valuing your work. Returns can come both financially and spiritually, and in many ways you do not yet realize. Open and realize your own needs on the physical level and realize the spiritual input to help these energies (which are) ready to take a leap to another plateau; but they are like a huge ball needing a shove up a hill to another level. Accept the help to reach new levels, where it has the ability to expand and cover even more

territory and reach many who otherwise could not feel this in their present life. Many are waiting for this probability to occur. (7/29/79)

Gay recognized what they had already discovered and tactfully inserted another belief they had not seen. They were afraid of "sacrificing individuality to a group." More people working with them meant an "organization" or "institution." That was a scary idea, but Gay was telling them that they could accept help and energy from others without giving up themselves.

They began using new affirmations in their daily meditation or self-hypnosis sessions. "I draw to me helpful, loving, positive people," and "I deserve to be helped." Feeling sure that this new programming would help, they went about their daily business. They had yet to deal with the emotional level of these beliefs.

A week after they began the new affirmations, they had scheduled three appointments: at 4 PM, 5:30 PM and at 8 PM. The earlier appointments were for people driving to Pennsylvania from Connecticut. At 4 PM, the women were at the office waiting. At 4:45 PM, they were still waiting. At 5 PM, they received word that the people coming were going to be another hour late. They had been delayed. They rushed home, rushed through supper, rushed back to the office, rushed through the two readings, then rushed back to Sandy's for the 8 PM appointment — fifteen minutes late. This had happened relatively frequently in the past year, and almost always with people traveling long distances to see them. It was very annoying, as they lost valuable time waiting; but it was also very hard to be openly angry, since the people came from such distances. Sheila always seemed to be more overtly annoyed during these times than Sandy. They had asked Gay about it. She said this would end when they valued their work more than they had so far. They answered, "Okay, Gay, but how?"

This particular evening, after finishing the last session, Sheila went home. A good friend, who happened to be a therapist, was staying with her at the time. Sheila was still fuming about the earlier events, and he suggested they explore the feelings. During the session, Sheila discovered more of her beliefs about trust — this time on a deeper, more emotional level. She felt that she *had to* give and give to others, but that she could not trust that anyone would do anything right for her—even be on time. This recent event had given her another opportunity to get in touch with the beliefs blocking her growth in an emotional way, which gave her release and a sense of peace. She felt she had let go of a lot of troublesome programming.

The night after all of this happened, Sandy had a similar emotional encounter as she meditated around 3 or 4 AM. She had found her meditations at that hour deeper and more satisfying than usual and her subsequent dreams clear and psychologically valuable. This particular night, before going to sleep, she gave herself the suggestion that she would wake up at 3 AM to meditate. She was tired, however, and felt she also needed sleep; so she did not set the alarm. At exactly 3 AM, the cat woke her, chasing a mouse through the television room. "I guess I'm supposed to meditate," she thought.

She very quickly went into a deep trance. She did her usual programming and began the affirmations, mentally repeating, "I draw to me helpful, positive, loving people" — two or three times. Then she began "I deserve to be helped." As she said these words in her mind, a wave of emotion washed over her body, and she began sobbing as the words "I deserve to be helped" reverberated through her head. The pain was realizing that she, Sandra Stevens, did deserve help from others. As the intensity of the feelings subsided, she heard a voice in her head telling her that this was her version of what Sheila experienced the night before. "You both need to value yourselves and your work." After a deep and peaceful sleep, she awoke feeling released and confident that the blocks created by these deep negatives would no longer stand in their way.

Beliefs are not bad. They are necessary for our physical existence. Awareness of beliefs as the building blocks of our physical reality gives us the personal power to create the kind of life we want to live. We all have the ability to weed out our limiting beliefs and expand our lives in many ways we may not yet realize.

Chapter 7

Thought Power:
HOW WE CREATE OUR REALITY
II

SCOTTSDALE, JULY, 1977. For five days, Sheila and Sandy had been immersed in new ideas – ideas telling them about the power of their thought. Each day as they returned from Dick Sutphen's lectures and hypnosis sessions, before lunch, before dinner, or during the mid-afternoon break, they would see a family of quail scurrying across their path near their room. Neither woman had ever been that close to these cute, little birds before. They found them adorable. Two adults and six or seven little fledglings. Now it was Saturday evening, and they were leaving the room to attend the closing function of the week-long seminar, a cocktail party. Gay had spoken to them that afternoon urging them to set aside their learning and problems and have some fun. She said she wanted a "good time" and explained that she experienced their reality through their vibrations – their thoughts and emotions. When they saw the birds once again, they began laughing and made a big fuss over them. "Look, Gay, see the birds! Aren't they cute? They're so adorable!" They were silly and enjoying it. They also enjoyed the party. Afterwards, they talked to Gay again and Sandy asked her if she had liked the quail.

> They are quite a family and sight. They go across the same time you come to your room and, if you notice, it is not always the same time, according to your concepts, that you walk to your room; but the quail run across for you, and you are here for them!

Sandy and Sheila had not given much thought to this "coincidence." The had accepted the gift of the quail sightings as part of the furnishings provided by the resort where they had been staying for the week. Gay was pointing out to them that if they had been a little more aware, they would have realized that this behavior was unusual for quail. The coincidences were too frequent and too inconsistent with normal time concepts. If they had seen the quail at the same chronological time each day, the event would not have seemed exceptional. However, that was not the case. Whenever they arrived at the room, at whatever time of the day it happened to be, the quail were scurrying across their path. It was they who had given themselves the "gift" of the quail – not the management of a well-run resort. Their enjoyment and subsequent emotional involvement with the little birds and their need for a dramatic lesson in creating reality had manifested the event.

Carl Jung, in his "Synchronicity: An Acausal Connecting Principle," calls this phenomena "synchronicity" – the connection between two events that is acausal in nature, but there because of its meaning to the person or persons experiencing the events. The quail scurrying by as Sandy and Sheila left their room in a regular manner took on special meaning for the women as they realized that it was their own feelings and emotions that brought about the "coincidence." During the next few years, the women learned that there are no "coincidences"; rather, every physical and psychic event has meaning at some level or another in terms of one's individual reality. The inner and outer realities of an individual are related. It is the inner thought, feelings, and emotions that "manifest" the outer physical reality. During the following day, Sandy and Sheila were to experience a "pile-up" of such "coincidences."

Sunday was to be their last full day in Arizona before returning home. They decided to rent a car and travel north to visit sights Dick Sutphen had talked about during the week. They had no set plan but intended to travel leisurely through some small towns and eventually reach Sedonia to experience the beauty of the red rocks and an energy spot Dick had told them about. During the week, much of the talk had been about "energy," "crystals," UFO sightings, Indian culture with its spirits and rituals, as well as general conversation about the beauty of Arizona's deserts and its wildlife.

The day began early. They left Scottsdale about 7 A.M., before breakfast, thinking they could get something to eat a little way down the road. They were unprepared for the vast emptiness between spots of civilization, as they were used to the East Coast with its chains of MacDonald's offering fast "doing it all for you" breakfasts. By 9:30, they were hungry. They had not even seen a billboard since leaving the confines of Phoenix's borders, so when they saw a little sign reading "Exit for Black Canyon City," they decided they would breakfast in that metropolis. Unfortunately, the only place open in this city of five or six broken-down old buildings was an unappetizing diner called the "Yellow Canary Restaurant." They drove by. As they stopped a little way down the road to turn around, however, they noticed a man waving his arms over his head in an attempt to get their attention. He was standing in front of the restaurant. Sheila looked at Sandy and shrugged. "I guess we're supposed to eat at the Yellow Canary."

They went back and met a delightful character named Frederick, who ended up telling them his life's story and how "they" were trying to take his wonderful restaurant away from him. Sandy realized she had some excellent story material for a book she had begun working on during the week. But, stranger still, during the time they were eating breakfast, only two other people entered the establishment – a cowboy and an older woman who must have been his mother. They went to the back and entered into an animated conversation with Frederick about "crystals" and "hot spots" where people would disappear if they were foolish enough to step on them. Sheila and Sandy stared at each other and held their laughter until they left. It was as if a parody of their week's learning had been played out in front of them.

After passing through Prescott, they found themselves crossing a flat valley between two mountains with wide stetches of desert on either side of the road. Sandy laughingly remarked that perhaps here she would see a roadrunner chasing a coyote. Her children had asked about this on the phone the previous evening. No sooner had she said the words than over to their right she saw a large coyote running toward them. She squealed and stomped on the brakes! No roadrunner, but sure enough! There was her coyote.

Crystal. All week they had heard about the mysterious power of crystal. Several of the women attending the seminar wore crystal jewelry. They had not seen crystal jewelry on the East Coast, but both women decided they would like some to wear. They had looked in the shops of Scottsdale but without success. They told themselves that it would just turn up. It did. Dick had suggested they visit the old mining town of Jerome, which he explained was now an artist's colony containing many shops owned by resident craftsmen. The first shop they entered in Jerome displayed a large variety of crystal jewelry and hanging crystal balls. Later they walked into an old dilapidated building which housed beautiful oil paintings of the Arizona landscape – each with a UFO floating somewhere in its sky.

Sandy had been thinking early in the week that she would like to see some Indian cave dwellings. She realized that they were too far north for Pueblo tribes and had accepted that it was not possible on this trip. Heading down the highway back toward Phoenix, she spotted a sign reading "Montezuma's Castle." She looked at Sheila and asked, "Should we?"

"Why not?" They pulled off the road, having no idea what Montezuma's Castle was. It was a six-hundred old cave dwelling of a long-lost Indian tribe.

Reaching Phoenix, after what had been a long and beautifully flowing day, Gay pulled one more "coincidence" for their fun and pleasure. It did not seem like fun at first, however, because they found themselves lost on the Phoenix side of Camelback Mountain, trying to reach the Scottsdale side. They were beginning to get irritated, as they were very tired. It was dark and late. Turning the car around, they looked behind themselves and found that they had travelled up the mountain and were overlooking the entire city of Phoenix with its beautiful night lights. Then they saw the street sign and knew Gay had a hand in their getting lost. They were on Arcadia Drive! Gay was always insisting that Arcadia was a "real" place where spirits play between lives.

Paying attention to "synchronicities," or meaningful coincidence, in our lives is one of the first steps to getting in touch with the power of our thought. These "coincidences" or "instant manifestations" allow us to see our thoughts materialize almost instantly. Viewed as significant, they are excellent examples which can later lead us to an understanding of how all of the events in our lives have their source in our thought. Sometimes the incidents are simply entertaining and fun. Sometimes they are lessons.

The following two incidents happened to Sandy just before this chapter was written. She was having lunch in a coffee shop, during her usual work day. She had ordered coffee with her lunch, but the waitress had forgotten to bring it. She finished lunch and impatiently checked her watch as the long invisible waitress reappeared from the kitchen. Seeing her annoyed customer, she rushed over, saying, "Oh, I forgot your coffee. I'll get it right away."

She rushed off and Sandy thought to herself, "She shouldn't charge me for that coffee. I had to wait too long."

The waitress returned, put down the coffee, picked up her bill and said, "I'm taking the coffee off your bill since you had to wait so long." Sandy stared at her with amazement.

The second incident was more of a lesson and illustrates the acceleration of learning that she and Sheila had been experiencing during the past year. Her children had missed their school bus, which meant that Sandy had to rush through her morning preparations in order to drive them to school on time and then reach her first morning's appointment on her job. She was very angry and did not want to yell at her sons as she felt like doing because they were already feeling guilty about missing the bus. But as she was driving them to school, her irritation mounted with each infraction committed by all the other drivers on the road. Normally, she takes such incidents in stride, as she drives most of her work day and finds that this part of her job flows smoothly. This particular morning the road seemed to be filled with irresponsible, crazy drivers. The accumulation of irritation finally turned to full-blown anger when a young man driving a truck pulled out in front of her, almost pushing her into the median of the road and causing an accident. He had not been paying attention to what he was doing. Sandy was furious and began honking her horn and mouthing her fury at the guilty young man. She was behaving in a manner she found repugnant during her calmer moments. She dropped the boys at school and continued on to work. Not ten minutes later, as she pulled from a left lane into a right lane, she heard honking behind her. She swerved back into the left lane just in time to miss hitting a car that had been slightly behind her on her right. Looking through the rear view mirror she could see a young woman shaking her fist and mouthing words of justifiable anger at her. Her own anger had just begun to subside and now she was the object of anger as intense as her own had been. She felt chastised and, as she thought over the incidents, she found meaning in the "coincidence." She had inappropriately dumped her unexpressed anger at her children on to the other drivers on the road, drawing to her potentially dangerous incidents. Being paid back in kind reminded her that anger, like all feelings, when expressed spontaneously and immediately, is natural and appropriate, but repressed and later released inappropriately can be possibly harmful. She marveled at the swiftness of the learning.

The women found that learning to use thought power could help in the practical aspect of their business. Their learning, however, came slowly and sometimes quite by accident. In the early fall of 1977, Sandy had her aura read at a psychic fair in one of the local malls near her home. The man told her some insightful and accurate details about her life; however, she thought he was totally wrong when he insisted that she would soon be involved in some kind of real estate dealings. She would move or sell real estate, he told her. She had no intention of doing either and just shook her head. When she and Sheila next met with Gay, she asked what he could have been talking about. Gay told them that they would be signing a lease for an office on the first of the new year. That seemed so far fetched that they laughed and forgot about the whole incident. In the meantime, Mind Matters was conceived and began to grow. Sheila decided that she would like a place to hold classes, as her apartment was too small and inconvenient for a suitable number of participants. She began to visualize in her mind the kind of place she would like to have. She took no action. Sometime around mid-December, a friend of hers remarked that there was an office for rent in a renovated barn just a mile down the road from her apartment. "Why not?" she thought and suggested to Sandy that they take a look. It was perfect. Two weeks later, on December 30th, they signed a lease for the office and Mind Matters had an official address.

We are always manifesting our reality. Everything in our lives is there because we put it there. Every person in our lives is there because we drew them there. Most of the time, we are completely unaware of when and how we do this. This unawareness leaves us at the mercy of emotions, beliefs, and thoughts that give us what we may not consciously wish in our lives. Once we become aware of this process, however, we can put the "laws" of manifestation to conscious use in our lives and be active participants in the forming of our personal reality. Sheila developed a noticeable talent for conscious manifestation, learning to satisfy her daily needs by using the power of her thought. This process does not operate in an objective, logical, and causal mode of consciousness. It develops out of an intuitive, "synchronistic" or connective mode of being-in-the-world. It is a talent gleaned from intuitively knowing the "connectedness" of things in the world. Recognize the intricacy of how everything "fits" and set aside the logical, expected have-tos and how-tos of conventional reality, and soon the playful freedom of creativity begins to drop whatever is appropriately desired into our laps.

Sometimes, to learn the process of manifestation, we find we must give ourselves great difficulties in order to exhaust all of the conventional methods of subsistence, to allow ourselves the experience of knowing the deepest source of our reality — our own thoughts and being-in-the-world. The conventional methods rely on cause and effect, logical, objective thinking, and action. Often these methods do not work. Paul Hawken's *The Magic of Findhorn* describes in painful detail the struggling of Peter and Eileen Caddy, founders of the community at Findhorn, Scotland, as they exhausted every conventional means of support before trusting enough to start using the principles of manifestation upon which Findhorn is based. Sheila went through a similar, if shorter, struggle herself during the winter of 1978-79.

Sheila had left her job with the welfare office during the early part of 1978. When she quit, she figured that she had just about enough money to see her through a year; and that is how long the money lasted.

In December of that year, she began to worry about money. Her bank book was hovering close to zero. Mind Matters was not bringing in enough to support her, and so she decided to get a part-time job in a toy shop during the Christmas season. She worked about three days, then she broke her foot. That brought more expense, as she was no longer covered by medical insurance. In January, she found herself home bound, unable to drive or even walk, with almost no source of income. Mind Matters had a few appointments scheduled, but the severe January weather often meant cancellations. She did not know how she was going to pay her February rent nor buy the few essentials she needed to get through the time it would take her foot to heal. There was no chance of finding a job in her physical condition.

She meditated. Someone had given her a book on color meditation. Choosing a color as a symbol for a quality desired in one's life, one could then visualize breathing in that color while meditating on it. Sheila chose a light, clear green for drawing abundance into her life. She meditated, breathing in the color. Then she let go. She trusted in manifestation and consciously gave up her own involvement in it. She had to — for, at this point, there was nothing else she could do.

A few weeks later — very close to her February rent due date — Sheila had lunch with a woman for whom she had done a reading the previous year. She had not seen the woman since the reading, but an unusual series of circumstances had brought them together now. The woman told Sheila that her reading had meant a lot to her. She had been meditating in the manner Gay had suggested and had contacted her own guide. She then said that she felt strange about something that had happened during one of her recent meditations. She said she had been thinking about Sheila and Sandy, and when in her mind, she reached her guide, he said, "Sheila needs money."

"Do you?" she asked. Sheila was shocked. She tried denying it, feeling embarrassed in front of this woman she hardly knew. The woman was reassuring, however, and told Sheila that she had some money and could give her whatever she needed at the present time, if she would accept it. The only condition was that the gift be anonymous and never mentioned to her again.

Sheila thanked her very much but said, "No, I'm fine. Don't

worry. I'll manage." She felt caught in a mesh of conflicting thoughts and feelings. She did need money. She had been meditating to draw the money she needed to her. She knew intellectually that the "laws" of New Age manifestation were to operate differently from the conventional methods of the past. But she had never taken anything, much less money, from a stranger before. She was fiercely independent and had always taken care of herself. She had worked for her money and believed that "good" people earned what they received. She also found that she could not quite believe that anyone — especially a stranger could be interested in helping her without an ulterior motive. For several days, these thoughts argued and fought within her consciousness. Outwardly, the snow got worse and most of the Mind Matters appointments for the week were cancelled. She finally had to come to terms with her beliefs and her situation. She cut through the old "programming" — the cultural "work ethic" beliefs, the false pride in her own independence, the disbelief that anyone would care enough about her to help her. The physical evidence was overwhelming — how the women received the information about her financial state, the broken foot, the cancelled appointments — all pointed to a new way of being, a new way to take care of her needs.

She called the woman and accepted the money. She got through the remainder of the winter. Her foot healed. The appointments increased once again and, in the early spring, she found a part-time job she enjoyed to supplement the money she earned with her readings and classes.

The experience was the beginning of a major shift in the way Sheila consciously related to her world. She found that by simply wishing, then trusting, all the physical needs of her life were met with an ease and simplicity she had never dreamed possible. Many of the material things she wanted, but had always thought required money were suddenly there. (Little things and big things.) She needed a pair of gloves. A day after thinking to herself that she would have to go to a store to buy some, she received a package in the mail from her mother who wrote, "I just thought you would like a pair of these nice driving gloves." This was an unusual event, as Sheila knew her mother's finances were limited. The same thing happened with a wallet she wanted. It was her birthday and she thought to herself, "Maybe someone will give me a wallet." Someone did. It was another package from her mother. Sometimes the things were not so small. She moved into a new apartment. Friends of hers were selling a large farmhouse and asked if she would be willing to "store" their expensive and beautiful stereo system. She could, of course, use the system during the two or three years they were away.

Bigger yet was her new car. Sheila had been driving an old, deteriorating Opel. She had paid $500 for it during the winter of 1978. It lasted a year and a half, but during the summer of 1979, she knew she would need a new one soon. She did not have enough money and wondered what she was going to do. "Something will turn up," she told herself.

Sandy drives a company car. She had not had to own a car during the five years she had worked for the pharmaceutical firm. During the summer of 1978, however, as she drove through the streets of Philadelphia, she spotted a newly painted red 1968 Volvo. It had a "For Sale" sign on it. It was inexpensive and looked beautiful. On an impulse, she stopped and bought it. She decided she wanted and could afford a car "of her own." The thought that she may someday leave her job was in the back of her mind, and she had been visualizing a pretty, little car like the one she was seeing. She loved the car and enjoyed driving it. During the year, she loaned it to a friend who, in exchange for its use, completely overhauled the engine, cleaning out all the accumulated ten years of potential problems. She was aware that Sheila needed a car, but neither woman thought about the Volvo. That was Sandy's toy and future investment.

Then, during the time that Sheila was reaching a crisis with her failing Opel, Sandy had a dream. She dreamt of her stepmother who had died ten years earlier. Sandy had loved her very much and now found that Ellie occasionally entered dreams and meditations with thoughts of encouragement and love. Sandy did not remember much of the dream, but the image of her stepmother's face was clearer than she could consciously remember experiencing it in years. When she awoke, she knew she was going to give the Volvo to Sheila. She was surprised that the thought had not occurred to her before this, but it did make sense. She wrote in her journal that day:

> I'm sure that this decision is Ellie's influence since she (Daddy?) gave me her car when she died. I also feel it's very, very unbalanced for me to have it when Sheila's driving an unreliable car. I don't need it, and it is excess baggage that could be holding me down.

After her stepmother had died unexpectedly, her father gave her Ellie's 1968 Volkswagon. She drove it until she went to work selling pharmaceuticals in 1976.

84   *Being Alive*

Sheila learned to give up needing to know how things were going to happen in her life. She learned to allow them to happen as they might. She examines her beliefs, sends out the thought, and then trusts — trusts that her needs will be met in whatever way is best and appropriate. She acts when opportunity is presented but does not worry about what she should be doing next to *make* things happen. That is, of course, when she's flowing with life and not fighting it. That flowing is more and more the reality of her life.

Sandy and Sheila are often in telepathic communication with one another. One will think that they need to talk, and then the phone will ring or the other will drive in the driveway. Incidents such as this have frequently occurred during the years they have been working together. Sometimes they have found that they each had the same idea at the same time about some project they were working on. Sometimes the "co-incidences" are funny. They began to realize that whenever they went out to dinner together, they always ordered the same food. It did not matter if other people were there or not — it was always the same; nor did it matter who ordered first. They became so self-conscious about this that they began choosing two alternatives, so that the second one ordering could quickly switch to a different entree. They laughed but often felt a silly loss of individuality. The thought power they enjoy together, however, usually works for the advantage of Mind Matters.

For the past couple of years, Sheila and Sandy had been teaching a day-long seminar they called "Creating Your Own Reality: A Seminar on Self-Hypnosis." This seminar was their most successful, filling even during times others did not. During the day, they progressively developed techniques for trance induction and a method for developing a "program" of affirmations and visualizations. Participants worked on a particular area of their lives that they wished to change and learned the steps they could take to get in touch with their beliefs in that area to develop counteracting affirmations and visualizations to reinforce the new programming in their subconscious. This procedure is specific and, when used regularly, is quite successful. Often Sandy and Sheila would learn months afterward from a participant how successful he or she had been with the "programming."

One woman, who had come to a seminar in the spring of 1978, turned up at a Christmas party they attended that year. They had not seen her since the seminar. She had wanted to learn how to program for a new job. She was a teacher who had been working in a small private school with children who had learning disabilities. Her work had been satisfying, but she felt it was time to move on. She wanted more money and an administrative position. She was very specific about what she wanted. She learned the self-hypnosis techniques and, as advised, did not concern herself with "how" it was to all come about. At the Christmas party, she enthusiastically told Sandy and Sheila that she had gotten exactly what she had programmed for.

The techniques that they taught during this seminar had also worked in their own lives – that is, until sometime during the latter part of 1978. The techniques were still valid. They were working for others and had worked for them, but something was wrong. The programs they were sending out were not "taking," and they both felt overwhelmed by the enormity of constantly assessing each and every aspect of their lives for new areas to "re-program." It was time for a change, but in what direction?

As is usual with the two women in times of mental crisis, a book fell into their hands. A good friend bought them each a copy of David Spangler's *The Laws of Manifestation*. This little book was written while David was co-director of Findhorn in Scotland. It was written in answer to a crisis in the spiritual community which had so successfully demonstrated the effectiveness of the techniques Sandy and Sheila had been teaching. The community had used "positive thought, precise formation of mental images with the consequent concentration of energy, faith and the bridging principle of putting God's will first."[1] It had worked. However, now it was time for a change.

Spangler introduced to the women the concept of "attunement" or being at one with the desired reality. It was time to let go of the specifics and move into a consciousness that concentrates on the qualities desired in life and trust that the specifics will follow naturally. This is what Sheila was learning with her physical manifestations. After reading Spangler's book and absorbing his ideas of attunement and manifestation, the women began using these principles in their own lives. About this time, Gay suggested that they meditate on the phrase, "I ask to be one with higher energies." They also began to meditate on the qualities they wanted in their lives, using affirmations such as "I ask to be one with peace" or "freedom" or "love" or "abundance." Whatever quality they currently desired in their lives became the object of their meditations. Sheila was practicing this concept when she did the color breathing in January of 1979, asking for abundance.

---

[1] David Spangler, *Vision of Findhorn Anthology,* (1976), p. 30.

In the late spring of that year, several people who had attended their self-hypnosis seminar and had been successfully using the principles they had learned, asked if Mind Matters could do an advanced self-hypnosis seminar—a refresher course. The women tucked the idea in the back of their minds for awhile. Pressure for this kind of seminar increased until finally they consented and scheduled a date. Neither of them had thought about what they would do in such a seminar, but Sheila assured Sandy, "Something will come up at the right time."

Sandy had been doing some personal work at the time on a long-time relationship that she wanted very much to succeed. A basic part of the potential success in the relationship had to do with her beliefs and concepts about freedom. She had been meditating on the concept of "freedom" and had been doing some visualization to cut the "controlling" links between this man and herself. She had been "seeing"—in her meditations—each of them free to come together and free to separate at will. Then one morning in a particularly deep trance, after doing the usual affirmations and visualizations, she "saw" the man and herself as two huge, pulsating cells in space. The cells were individual and freely floating, like amoebas in water seen through a microscope. Other times they would merge, but then they would separate. She experienced joy in both. She also had been using the affirmation "I am one with higher energies," as well as asking for the qualities she desired in her life, such as freedom, peace, love and creativity. The emotional intensity of experiencing the cells signaled to her the potential for a new kind of freedom in her relationships. She then found that she began to merge with the qualities she desired and her internal statement became "I am free, peaceful, loveable and creative." A few days later, after repeating the visualizations, she found that, rather than just describing herself as free or peaceful or loveable, she actually moved into attunement with the qualities – she merged and became one with what she wanted. As the words "I am freedom," "I am peace," "I am love," came without effort or planning, her mind began to play with the concrete images associated with these qualities in her physical life.

The entire process had simply flowed through her meditations, and when she came out of trance she knew what the new seminar would be like. She called Sheila and they talked about how they could use this process to design an advanced self-hypnosis seminar. Sheila immediately understood and knew how she would contribute to the seminar. She had been learning in a very physical way what Sandy had experienced in meditation. Both of their lives had been changing with these new ideas, and the natural result was a new offering from Mind Matters. Sandy designed the hypnosis sessions to lead the participants from specific programming to attunement. Sheila gathered the verbal and intellectual material to prepare the lecture and discussion sessions. The seminar was a success. Their attunement with each other has often led to such creative results.

What we are to receive in the future is that which we are "seeing" in our present. Gay has always stressed awareness of the present when people would ask her about their future. She seldom makes predictions. When she does, it is always with the qualification that the future is open: it is the creativity of every person to make his or her own life, drawing from an infinite number of probabilities, each waiting to be actualized in a specific time-and-space focus. In order to manifest the future we want, it is important to be completely aware of our present. In October of 1978, Gay said the following to Sandy and Sheila:

Gay: Future is often seen as symbols and, like the morning fog, lifts and is clear later in the day.

Sandy: Do we fail to see the future because we are so wrapped up in the present that only by hindsight do we see what was happening?

Gay: You are clouded not because you are in the middle of the present, but because you are unaware of the present. To be totally in the present includes an awareness of the future, but the future is many possibilities. Just as the day's weather is not clear at the beginning, then the fog lifts and you see.

Sandy: As we become more in the present, then the future is more obvious?

Gay: Yes. Still, you can change or alter it. Knowing helps you do so.

During a reading that same year, Gay said the following to a businessman from Philadelphia:

You can predict future events by staying totally in the present and realizing there is no future, and there are many probabilities to explore in your so-called future. If you can begin to focus on the present only, you will have a good sense of the strongest probability now, and there is no future to concern yourself with. This is one thing that does strongly motivate you—a need to control what will happen to you, and to know what is to be. What is to be is now, and this is all there is – only now. You are too concerned with the future and its implications for you.

Living totally in the present, being aware of thoughts, feelings, emotions, and attuning to the qualities we want in our lives will assure that our future will gradually flow into a Now that is fulfilling and beautiful.

Chapter 8

"Past" Lives?

SANDY'S BODY FELT HEAVY. She was aware of everything around her—Sheila laying somewhere off to her right, the hundred or so other people spread out and behind her throughout the huge ballroom, the hardness of the floor, the annoying cough of a man a few feet away, and the sound of Dick Sutphen's voice as he commanded her and all of these other people to go "deeper and deeper into this relaxing, peaceful hypnotic trance." She had prepared for this moment, using the conditioning tape Sutphen had sent her as part of a preparatory kit for the seminar. She was conditioned to his voice even though this was the first day she had seen the man. Even with that conditioning, however, she had her doubts about whether this whole thing would work. Maybe for others, but her? She wasn't sure how she felt about the whole business of reincarnation anyway.

Gay had been telling her about her past lives for seven or eight months now; but that had been fun — a way to help explain certain feelings or experiences, perhaps — but it was still an intellectual exercise for her. She listened to Gay and she read about others' experiences and theories, but having past lives was not real to her yet. But here she was, and Dick was still counting down, "number one, you are now in the deepest possible hypnotic trance...." He then began taking them back through their present life experiences. Sandy saw herself at age ten and age five with no difficulty, but those were conscious memories. That was easy. Nothing new came up. No old, forgotten memories sprang up to surprise her and convince her that indeed, as Dick had suggested, "every thought, every action, from this life and every life you've ever lived are recorded in the memory banks of your subconscious mind." They were just plain old ordinary memories.

Then Dick began to take them back through the womb. Sandy became very uncomfortable. She wanted out. She could not see herself in her mother's womb, and she was having terrible feelings — feelings of being suffocated and of being unwanted. She wanted out and was relieved when Dick finally gave the order to go back even further in time: to "another time and another place where, on the count of one, you will step into a light and find yourself in a previous lifetime at the age of fifteen." Sandy heard the instructions. So relieved to be out of that uncomfortable womb, she ceased worrying about whether or not the process was going to work. Suddenly Dick was saying, "number one, you are now there. You are now fifteen years old in another time and another place. Perceive yourself. And trust your mind."

The room and all the people around her were gone. Sandy found herself on a sunlit street high up in a city that was overlooking a beautiful blue sea. She could look far down through the buildings to the sea. This was not a place that she had ever seen in her present life. She also realized that she was conscious of being two people at once. She was herself with her Sandy-thinking mind; but she was also a young, handsome black-haired boy wearing knee-length, white draw-string pants and a loose white cotton shirt. The boy seemed very annoyed that he was "stopped" on the street. Sandy felt that he wanted to continue running down the street toward the sea but that she had in some way stopped him. She was fascinated by the whole scene. It was so real. Meanwhile Dick was asking her to answer questions in her mind about places, dates, and so on. But she was much too taken with the entire scene to be concerned with such mundane details. She was very aware of the boy's desire to be free to explore the streets of his city. She got the feeling that he was not able to do so as often as he would like and now here she, or something he could not explain, was holding him in place. She seemed unable to let him go and move about. Later, she felt sure that she would recognize the scene. It was so vivid. The sharpness of this first regression stayed with her throughout the remainder of the week. And although she was to have many future experiences with other past times and places, with more complicated psychological dramas and emotional scenes, nothing else remained as sensually alive as that first step into another lifetime.

Why do this? Why had Sheila and Sandy travelled across the country to lay on this ballroom floor, to join this large group of people as they moved through layers of memory to times and places far away from Scottsdale, Arizona in 1977? Most of the people there were experiencing, as Sandy had, many new realities. Sutphen talked about the effects of "karma" — what he called "past programming" — from one's present life and past lives which effect present reality. He repeatedly insisted that "wisdom erases karma" and that wisdom could result from bringing buried memories to conscious awareness.

Then a "letting go" could happen and positive change could occur in people's everyday lives. Sandy and Sheila understood what he was talking about, although they also understood that the process of "letting go" was often slower and more painful than perhaps Sutphen was implying. They had examined the memories of their present lives thoroughly during their three and a half years of intensive therapy which had emphasized the value of reliving traumatic childhood events in order to become fully conscious of the influences these events had on the present. This process had worked well for them. The changes in their lives – particularly in how they felt about themselves – had come about slowly but in very tangible ways that they, at least subjectively, could measure.

So there were several reasons why they lay on that ballroom floor. One was their faith in the process – a faith that had come from their own experience. Confirmation of their new discoveries about the possible nature of reality was another. Sutphen's book, *You Were Born Again to Be Together,* discussed many of the same ideas that Gay had been suggesting to them. Curiosity about the experience of past-life regression, actually seeing and feeling where they may have lived before, attracted them – especially Sandy. These feelings and concepts were still new to her. Sheila had felt them all her life, and for her it was all a "Yes, of course, this is the way it is" recognition of reality. The week was also a vacation, a time of fun and play. It was fun and the play was serious. During the week, they were exposed to many new ideas and concepts that they later continued to explore and study. Eventually these studies coalesced into the systems of metaphysical thought that underlie the work they do with Mind Matters and the ideas presented in this book.

Both women underwent many regressions in Arizona and later at home. While they were learning to be regressive hypnotists themselves, they naturally used each other as subjects. They found regression valuable in resolving conficts that they were unable to trace to present life trauma.

Sheila had grown up with a fear of being tested. Because of this fear when in school she received consistently poorer grades than she should have. She did fine in class discussions or on papers written at home. She knew the material that was expected by her teachers but, whenever she was confronted with a test or final examination, she would freeze, her mind would blank, and she would hand in an incomplete or poorly done paper. It mattered little whether the specific teacher was understanding and sympathetic or impatient and harsh.

The result of test taking was always the same — disastrous. In her adult life, she avoided situations in which she might be tested. Consequently, many areas of her life became awkward and painful. She had uncovered nothing during her therapy that would explain the extent of the problem.

The issue began to enlarge when she started doing readings for people. She would become so anxious before a reading that she often wondered whether or not she really wanted to be doing that kind of work. Gay kept reassuring her that she need do nothing except get out of the way and allow her to speak the words, but Sheila was still frightened because she was involved intimately with the process and ultimately responsible for the words — at least in a physical world sense. The problem finally gave her so much distress that Sandy suggested they do a regression to see if they could alleviate it.

They had asked Gay about the problem while they were in Scottsdale during July, 1977. Sutphen had given the participants of the seminar an ESP test, using an hypnosis technique, so that people could experience their psychic abilities. Sheila, who had been easily demonstrating psychic talents for a long time, froze and was unable to perform the simple test. She was very upset about it and so they consulted Gay:

> The test was connected with a death. Executed in 1421 in Spain...
> her enemies plotted a test they designed to fail....It was set up so
> she couldn't possibly pass the test.

She suggested that Sheila undergo a regression to relive this experience. When the number of their readings began to increase and Sheila's distress rose, Sandy suggested that it was time to try.

When Sheila came out of the time tunnel, at Sandy's verbal command, she found herself in darkness. During regressions Sheila usually has feelings rather than visualizations. She has a sense of "knowing" what is happening and very intensely feels the emotional climate of the situation. Now she was caught in something, bound tightly, and in total darkness. She realized she was underground, in some kind of hole, and had been there for what felt like a long time. She was very frightened. Sandy quickly moved her ahead to the time when she was to be released from the hole. She then described herself being pulled out and carried, blindfolded, to a prison. Sandy questioned her about her circumstances. She was in Spain during the time of the Spanish Inquisition. She was male, a leader of a small group of religious dissidents. She was taken to a place where she was continually questioned about her beliefs and activities. Later she was taken to a public square where she was tied to a wheel-like structure. All of the villagers were gathered around her. The people who had captured her then began to ask her questions that had answers which were wrong no matter how she answered. She began to realize that this was done for the benefit of the public; she was to be disgraced so that all the work she and her group had done would be discredited. It worked, and as the "trial" drew to an end, Sheila, lying on Sandy's couch in trance, began to become extremely agitated and scared. Sandy removed her from the situation to a "higher self" perspective, where she could describe what happened from a detached point of view without experiencing the physical and emotional pain. Sheila described how the villagers were instructed to stone her as the wheel to which she was tied slowly turned round and round. It was a slow and violent death.

The aspect of Sheila who had experienced the death had been unable to see that he had been set up. He was too close to the situation. Sheila, however, from her Twentieth Century perspective, could see clearly what had happened. There was no way she could have passed a "test" that was no more than a public display for the purpose of discrediting her work. Not realizing this, she had continued throughout her present life to be influenced by the memory of not having done something right. It was this fear that immobilized her. Re-experiencing the entire trial and death from a detached perspective released her from the influence and the belief that she could not perform in test situations. The readings became much easier, and a year or two later, when confronted with a testing young man who had come with his girlfriend to her reading, Sheila responded to his goading with confidence and emotional control, asking him to leave so that they could get on with their session. After this, she turned to Sandy and remarked, "I would never have done that before resolving that testing thing. I would have believed his criticisms and judgments about what I was doing. Thank goodness."

Sheila was helped with another psychological problem through past-life information: her ambivalence about the possibility of being a mother that she had experienced during her marriage. She had tried to find reasons for this ambivalence in therapy. Her only insight was that she felt sure that if she did agree to have the children her husband wanted, he would take them away from her. She was unable to find any objective reason for feeling that way. Nothing in her childhood pointed to such a belief. She was the third of four children all raised by her mother and father. Her father died when she was fifteen, but the family had been conventionally stable and intact until that time. Her mother continued to keep the two younger children together until Sheila left for college.

When she and Sandy began talking to Gay, Gay described the life they had shared in Wales during the Eighteenth Century where they had known her. They frequently questioned Gay on the Ouija Board about the details of this life. Gay told Sheila about a child that she had had out of wedlock while still living in the small Welsh village. She and Sandy had subsequently run away from the village to go to London to live. When Sheila asked Gay what had happened to her baby when she left the village, Gay told her that her parents had taken the child away, declaring her an unfit and immoral mother, and refusing to allow any further contact. Gay said that this had happened repeatedly to Sheila in other lifetimes and was an influence now. It did seem to explain her reluctance to become a mother, even though at times she had wanted a child very much. Then during a reading she had been doing for a good friend soon after they began their work, Sheila had what could be called a spontaneous regression and experienced one of those situations to which Gay had referred.

Sheila was in a usual state of trance, conscious of Gay's words but somewhere off to the side. Gay was explaining to the woman why she had always had feelings that she should have been a boy. Gay told her that she had been born into an African tribe centuries ago where males were valued but baby girls were unwanted. The boys were raised to be warriors; but when the supply of girls outweighed the tribe's need for reproduction, they were killed in order not to have to be fed and cared for. As Gay spoke, Sheila suddenly became overwhelmed with emotion, crying and feeling much sadness and loss, experiencing horror of the actual slaughter of these babies. Her feelings were very strong — stronger than any empathy she might usually feel for a client and friend. After she calmed down, she went back into trance and Gay explained that at one time Sheila had been the mother of one of these baby girls.

During the writing of this chapter, Sandy was witness to what Jane Roberts calls a "reincarnational drama."[1] Sheila and Sandy were scheduled to do a reading for a man Sheila had met about a month before. He had come into the restaurant in which she was working and had asked her to dinner and later to a movie. She told Sandy that he was very nice and had talked to her at length about a long but shaky relationship he had had with a woman. She assumed that was why he

---

[1] *Adventures in Consciousness*, Chapter 2.

had made the appointment for the reading. When he arrived, Sandy found him pleasant and easy to talk to. He seemed enthusiastic about talking to Gay. He said he had been drawn to Sheila the first time he saw her; and as soon as she told him about Gay, he had wanted an appointment immediately and was disappointed that he had to wait a week before coming. Sandy thought to herself that his reading would flow easily and quickly because of his attitude. That, however, was not to be.

They sat down and poured the tea. Sandy turned to the man, as she usually did, and asked if he had any specific questions that he wanted Gay to address. "No, I just want her to talk to me about me."

That was okay. Often people came who made such a request and the session would flow easily. As they experienced the kind of material Gay delivered, they would often begin to ask questions or comment on what they were receiving and how it applied to their lives. Sheila was sitting cross-legged on the couch as she went into trance. Gay began by telling the man that he had indeed been drawn here and she would explain why. She then started to give him metaphysical concepts about manifesting reality and work done in dream states. This was unusual, but occasionally someone would come for a session who had no previous experience with metaphysics, but whom Gay felt had an innate understanding, usually gleaned from past experience; and so she would speak in these terms, sure the person would understand at deeper levels. She told him that he had lived in Wales in the Eighteenth Century. She also said that she had been in his dreams. Sandy realized that this was one of the rare people who occasionally appeared whom Gay had known her own previous lifetimes. This had only happened about three times since they had begun three years before – three out of some four hundred sessions. Her curiosity was piqued. Sandy asked Gay for more information on the Wales life and whether or not this man had known her personally. She answered that he had, for the village was very small and everyone knew the others as friends and neighbors. She then abruptly reverted back to his work, which she had been discussing before Sandy's question. The first trance was of normal length.

During the break between trances, Sheila asked him if the material was of help and whether he now had any questions. He replied that it was all very "interesting" but did not tell him anything new, and "No," he did not have any questions. "I just want her to tell me about me," he insisted again, strongly implying that Gay had not given him what he wanted.

Sandy noticed that he was sitting with his arms and legs crossed and thought to herself that he was resisting. "That's his choice," she thought. "He'll get as much as he is open to." That attitude had been a difficult lesson for the women to learn when they were beginning, as they both had a need to satisfy people and would often try hard to please everyone who came. They had learned that the kind of communication in which they were engaged involved cooperation among all the different energies in the room. The more those seeking help from Gay gave of themselves to Sheila and Sandy through their willingness to be open and communicative, the more insight they would receive from Gay. They had also found that most of the few resistant people who had come to them over the years eventually acknowledged hearing what they needed at the time, even if it was that they were closed and unreceptive to communication. This had given the women confidence and had freed them from the need to try to please those who could not be satisfied. Interestingly, in the next trance, Gay spoke to the man about "trusting" and "asking" for what he needed. Her last sentence in what was an unusually short trance was: "No communication is in one direction but it is a co-creative act."

Again, Sandy asked him if he had any specific questions for Gay. His answer was the same as before and his attitude was the same. He insisted that he wanted to hear what she had to say or he would not be there, but the implication was that she was not saying anything that was particularly pertinent to him. Sandy noticed that Sheila was becoming strained. She knew these kind of readings drained her energy, but she was confident that Sheila could see that the problem was his and detach herself from the situation. She, herself, began to feel quite indifferent to the entire session and began to wish it would hurry and end so she could go to bed. It had been a long day and this session was not interesting enough to keep her attention or renew her energy.

The third trance was also short. Gay touched somewhat on the man's relationships with women, but again, his attitude remained closed and resistant. After the trance, Sheila began talking to him in a quiet, controlled voice. At first, Sandy was not tuned into what Sheila was saying because she felt indifferent and impatient toward the entire session, but suddenly she heard Sheila saying words to the effect that if this was not the right night for the reading, perhaps they could do it another time. Sandy came to attention. What in the world was Sheila talking about? They had already devoted an hour to this impossible young man who was giving them so little! "The material is good," she thought. "It's not our fault he can't take it in."

She listened to Sheila now and began to note that, in a very controlled way, Sheila was extremely agitated. She was explaining that she felt the man's resistance, and so it was very difficult for her to be doing the reading: "I know you really want to talk to Gay," she was saying, "but I feel this wall around you that I simply can't penetrate. You want to be open, but at a very deep level, there's this wall, and I keep bumping into it. I wouldn't want you to pay for something...."

Here Sandy, in her detached and still practical non-involvement, thought, "Wait a minute. Not pay for this! What is she talking about? I've never seen her do this before." She looked closely at Sheila and began to "see" that there was much more going on than was usual under the circumstances. Sheila was very upset. In fact, Sandy had not seen her so upset in a long time. The man was still sitting there with his arms and legs crossed. The two of them were engaged in an intense, emotional conversation that seemed to her to be completely at cross-purposes. Sheila was talking about him being closed and behind a wall, and that she was having feelings that were interfering with the quality of the session (Sandy did not believe this was objectively true — the material had been quite good). He was insisting that he really did want the session and had come in good faith. They kept going round and round, saying the same words over and over. Sandy, now very alert, could see that they were communicating at several levels at the same time. She could almost "see" the intensity that locked them together. It was as if they were "caught" in a drama that went far deeper than the actual events occurring in the room. Sandy remembered what Gay had said earlier about Wales. She turned to the man and said, "If you would sit back and uncross your arms and legs and ask a question, you will get what it is that you want."

He looked startled as if he had had no idea that his body was so closed. He immediately uncrossed his arms and legs and began to talk about what was really on his mind. To Sandy, it was as if she were watching a flower unfold. Once his question was asked, she knew that Gay could help him.

Sheila, however, was still caught in her feelings. She had not yet been able to see that a change had taken place, and began to feel that she could not go on. Her energy was drained, and she looked exhausted. Sandy knew they had to finish this — whatever it was that was happening. She told Sheila what she had been "seeing" — the different and deeper levels of communication – and that she felt the entire situation was somehow connected to the village in Eighteenth Century Wales. She suggested that Sheila lie down and put herself into the deepest possible trance, setting herself aside as much as possible, "letting Gay do it all," as she had done in earlier sessions. Sheila agreed to try. The last trance fit together the pieces in what had turned out to be a very unusual and dramatic evening:

> Yes, there is a deeper connection and communication here. There is a lack of trust in women in general, not of me but of the woman Sheila was in Wales. Regan was her name. As I said, you were a woodworker and you knew this woman well. Your life was closely allied to the church, and you followed its rules quite to the letter. Although there was an attraction to Regan, it was not acted upon; and you were quite shocked many years later to hear of her life in London. There was also a child born in the village, and the father was not known. You had many desires kept closely under control by the church and your upbringing, and I feel that there was a lack of trust here for you wanted her to be something that she was not. There is a tendency for you to place women on pedestals much higher than they can ever hope to be, and then you are quite disappointed and angry when they are not what you expect....(3/4/80)

Gay went on to talk to him about his beliefs and anger toward women in general and what he could do about it. At the end of the trance, he was dazed but excited about what had happened. He repeatedly said that Gay had given him even more than he had ever expected.

Sandy asked Sheila how she felt. "Exhausted but relieved," she replied. It took them both a couple of days to realize the impact of the experience.

Sheila hardly knew the man. She did not feel emotionally involved with him in any way before the reading. There were no early indications in their interactions to predict the intensity of the emotional exchange that occurred during the evening. During the exchange, Sheila did not maintain her usual objectivity and composure but became completely caught up in the emotional drama – an "emotional" drama because it had no apparent corollary to her physical life, but was real and happening just the same. After Gay spoke the last trance, it became apparent that the intensity of the feelings and the behavior each of them – Sheila and the man – were experiencing were dictated, not by their present Twentieth Century selves, but by other aspects of themselves that had once lived in Eighteenth Century Wales.

Sheila's feelings of being tested, of not being good enough, of having more expected of her than she could possibly be, were called forth by this man, who came with his own past feelings and beliefs.

When Sandy typed the reading, she realized that throughout the entire session there were clues leading up to the final drama. The man had been "drawn" there and, indeed, had even said himself that he had felt "drawn" to Sheila. Gay had been in his dreams as he had, at unconscious levels, asked for guidance. "There is no separateness," she told him in the second trance. "You are not isolated or alone as you sometimes enjoy believing that you are." The connections between him and Sheila had certainly illustrated that statement. Their past connections had, under the pressure of the situation, intruded upon their present reality until they were no longer relating as the two individuals they thought they were. People are not separate and alone but interconnected and related. The drama had also given Sandy and Sheila another example of how real the influences from "other" realities are in our daily lives — how much they effect our feelings and interactions with others. If we are not aware of these influences, then it is little wonder that many of us feel "out of control" and powerless over the circumstances of our lives.

Back in August of 1977, Gay had said the following to Sandy and Sheila in answer to a question about cause and effect in past-life situations:

> As you are beginning to become aware, all is now. Cause and effect don't exist. Now is all. You can see how important now is. It means your control of past and future is now. Right now. (How do we get our beliefs if not from past experiences?) You need to learn just that all is now. I know it makes no sense to you. It will. I see no sense going into many words. Just all is now.

It was certainly true that they did not understand how reality could not include cause and effect. The concept of simultaneous time and space was being presented to them over and over. Intellectually neither of them questioned their reading of Seth or Sutphen (and much later the writers of "new physics" in books such as *Space-Time and Beyond, The Tao of Physics,* and *The Dancing Wu Li Masters*), but understanding this idea on an experiential level was something else indeed. They lived in a reality of time and space. That happened, then this, and on and on, from one event to another, in their daily lives. Occasionally in meditative or dream states of consciousness, they would receive glimpses of realitites not defined by sequential time but by different rules and different perimeters. Their awareness increased gradually, however, and by the time the above incident occurred in the winter of 1980, both women had developed an innate understanding of this concept, gained through experience rather than any empirical process. Reincarnation was no longer a sequential progression through many lifetimes, each building on the other, accruing reward and punishment through the actions of each individual. Rather, a more dynamic concept had emerged through their learning – a reality of consciousness and relatedness where awareness of the richness of our beings and the dynamics of our interactions brings us to a new kind of freedom. During a reading for a woman in August of 1979, Gay said the following:

> First, I would like to begin by explaining what the influence from a previous lifetime means, for I feel that you have beliefs about needing to be punished and beliefs that you are a bad person.... Other lifetimes are influencing you, but they are not you. There is not one continuous stream of consciousness called you, but there is only you as you exist now, separate and unique from the other aspects of yourself. You are not the same you as I will describe being in another life. The future, past, present all have equal influences on each other. It is very important to give abundance and joy to yourself now for this is all that exists. In giving to yourself, you free the other aspects of yourself. Past lives are simply lifetimes that represent close psychic connections to your greater soul. They are not you but influence you. By becoming aware, then, all that is necessary is to let go of the negatives by sending these parts of you love, or incorporating the many positives. The influence does not move in a straight line from the negative to constant improvement; but the influences spread out like a wheel in many different directions.

   Very early in their learning, Sheila and Sandy had encountered phenomena which shook up whatever conventional ideas about reincarnation they had. Before going to Sutphen's seminar in July of 1977, two incidents occurred that seemed strange and "out of order."
   One Sunday afternoon in April, Sandy had returned from an excursion to a flea market. It was a warm day and she felt lazy and sleepy. She laid down on her bed and drifted into a trance state just bordering on sleep. She began experiencing a lot of images. While her active mind usually works on a top level, often during trance, her mantra takes over. Then she is conscious of dramas occurring in the

deeper levels of her mind. This was happening now and she became aware of several phenomena going on at once. Her body began to lighten, and she felt that now familiar feeling of energy moving up through her body. It first settled in her chest. She took a deep breath and held it there. The sensation was pleasurable. She felt attached to her body at her chest and head and yet out of it at the same time. Then the energy moved into her head. She began receiving new, overlaying images, one of her older son and the other of a foggy land with mountains. Thin waif-like forms in grey gowns and turbans were walking, or rather moving, through the air. Sandy could not determine whether they were happy or sad. Then she got a sudden flash that she had completely left her body and she "realized" that she was with a young dark-haired man who was trying hard to sit up in what was his sick bed. He wore pajamas. Sandy told him he must not get up, that it was important that he lie down and relax. He needed rest. She seemed to know what his situation was. She kept reassuring him and found that she identified with him in some way. She felt a pain in her shoulder, which at first startled her, but she immediately felt calm as she realized it was *his* pain. All of this drama was going on behind her conscious mind, which had let go of her mantra, had speculated on what was happening, and then gave her and the young man reassurance that everything was okay. When she came out of the trance, she found herself feeling light but good.

The next morning, during her meditation, she again found herself wandering through hospital corridors, and then, once again, in the room with the young man who was lying still and very sick. She again felt the need to help him.

That evening she and Sheila had a session on the Ouija Board with Gay. She asked who the young man in her meditation was:

Gay: ALTER EGO
Sandy: Where is he?
Gay: HAITI
Sandy: How can I help him?
Gay: SPIRITUALLY
Sandy: What do you mean by "alter ego"?
Gay: OTHER PART OF U
Sandy: How is he spiritually in trouble?
Gay: MIND SET BACKWARDS A WAY BACK NOT NOW
Sandy: Is he alive now?
Gay: YES

Sandy: What do you mean then?
Gay: TIME. CONFUSED ABOUT REALITY
Sandy: Is he mentally ill?
Gay: THEY SAY SO
Sandy: How can I help him?
Gay: U DONT DO ANYTHING BUT HELP URSELF. HE WILL BENEFIT.

They did not understand what it was all about, but filed it away in their consciousness as new — to be understood later, maybe.

Then in July, just before they were to leave for Arizona, another incident happened of the same nature. Sandy's son, Steven, had been feeling mopey for several days. There was nothing wrong physically, but his mood was down, and he seemed very tired and low on energy. He had agreed to help with the Ouija Board that night so Sandy could take down the letters as they came through. After Gay signaled her presence, Steven asked why he had been feeling sick lately?

Gay: ZEKE DOES
Steven: Who is Zeke?
Gay: STEVE OTHER SELF
Steven: Is there anything I can do to not feel bad?
Gay: JUST CING THIS WILL HELP. ALSO ASK FOR NOMAN (his guide) BEFORE FALL ASLEEP.
Sandy: Is Zeke a person alive now?
Gay: YES
Steven: Where does he live?
Gay: TEXAS   DALLAS
Steven: How old is he?
Gay: 79   LUNGS VERY BAD
Sandy: Can you explain how he is connected to Steven?
Gay: OTHER SELF. SOUL HAS PARTS MAKING WHOLE. NOT UNUSUAL TO BE IN MORE THAN ONE PERSON.

Here again they were confronted with a new idea. Could a soul be exploring more than one physical body at any given time? Is this what Gay was telling them? This Zeke person was certainly having a negative effect on Steven's health. Sandy wondered what effects the man in Haiti had had on her moods in the past?

A few days later they were to learn about Gay's "other selves" from Dick Sutphen. A few months later they were to read a similar theory from Seth in a new Jane Roberts book. Dick calls this phenomena "parallel lives" and describes in detail his discovery of the idea in his book, *Past Lives, Future Loves.* He had repeatedly encountered overlapping times and dates with regressed subjects whom he felt were genuinely experiencing past lives. He too had set the "problem" aside and eventually, through his own higher self and his wife, Trenna's, mediumship, developed the concept of "parallel lives." Shortly after that time, Seth presented the same idea in *Unknown Realities,* Vol. I & II, calling the various physical explorations "counterparts." Dick developed an hypnosis technique to take his seminar participants to these "parallel" realities to experience who they were or had been during their present lifetimes, in addition to who they were now. As Dick began presenting these ideas, leading up to that hypnosis session, Sandy and Sheila began to realize that they had already encountered the concept of parallel realities. In fact, shortly before attending the session, Gay had told them that Steven would be feeling better now for Zeke had died. (Sandy did call home later to see if that was so and indeed Steven reported "feeling fine." Sandy did not tell him of Gay's news.)

During the parallel-life hypnosis session, Sandy again found herself with the young man. This time, however, she was not in a hospital but in a cabin in some mountains. She was sure the place was Puerto Rico, however, and not Haiti, although she did not know why she was sure. She could see the man as he sat at a desk writing. She felt as if she was floating in the air near the ceiling looking down at the top of his head. She felt quite surprised to be there, as she had not thought about him before the session. She and Sheila had been conscious only of Zeke and his influence on Steven. Sandy found that she could engage in a mental "conversation" with the young man, although he did not seem to be consciously aware of her presence. He "told" her that he was better now and that he "remembered" her as the woman who had come to him when he was in the hospital in Haiti. He had had a schizophrenic breakdown but was better now. He gave her some facts about his life – his name, the name of his psychiatrist, some information about his parents. After this, Sandy "re-lived" the experience that had occurred in April, lying on her bed, except that this time she was seeing it from his viewpoint. She saw herself approach him as if he were having a vision or hallucination. She felt as if she had lost contact with reality and was floating in and out. Her thinking was disorganized and choppy. After the scene died out, she again felt fine.

Since that time, Sheila and Sandy have learned much about

"other selves" and their influence on our lives. Gay had insisted that they were no more or less an influence than any other, whether it be a past life, future life, or the effects of thoughts of those around us. Awareness, however, of these influences can free us of their effects in the same way that awareness of present-life trauma, or past-life trauma, can open us to letting-go. This process of letting go then frees us to create the reality that we desire in our present focus. Sending love to any aspect of ourselves that may be troubled, past, present or future, helps the total being.

As the concept of "other selves" began to show up in various readings and class discussions, people began to be concerned about the influence of these "other" people on their lives. Usually the immediate assumption was that the affect had to be negative. Gay continues to stress that influences simply are, and whether they are negative or positive is determined by the consciousness of the individual. One woman coming for a reading found that having an "other self" could be a helpful, freeing experience. She had been caught in a destructive relationship with a man for a long time and had been exhausted by the effort taken to free herself. She still doubted her strength, afraid of his power to change her decision to be away from him. She was also a person who usually felt that she had to do everything by herself. Gay said to her:

> There is another self who is having an influence on you. It is a
> woman who is around   now and she is helping you to free
> yourself from him for she is a very spiritual, positive individual
> who recently returned from India and is in a very bright place. She
> is not letting him affect her, and this is helping you. She is simply
> living near him and not a lover but seeing him with compassion —
> not being affected. I feel her as a great help to you. (2/21/79)

Under Dick Sutphen's direction that week in July, 1977, Sheila and Sandy explored many new realities. They progressed into a future life, frequency switched into alternate realities, and moved into their own higher self for what was then a new perspective on their total being. Sutphen describes all of these techniques and the rationale for these experimental hypnotic sessions in his book, *Past Lives, Future Loves*, published some two years after the 1977 sessions. For the two women, the experience expanded their concepts of who they were and gave them direction for their own explorations. Later, after they had trained to become regressive hypnotists with Sutphen, they explored probable lives, as well as past and future lives, using Seth's concepts.

These private sessions proved useful personally and again expanded their concept of "reincarnation." They began to use the word "influences" rather than "past lives" when referring to the effects of our total being on our present focus.

There are many new theories to explain reincarnation. Sutphen's books explain his various ideas, as well as David Palladin's concepts as he channels for Kandinsky. Richard Bach's book, *Illusions,* presents the idea of reincarnation as illusion: a series of movie houses, each playing a different picture, each of us becoming "lost" in the one we have chosen at any given second, although all are playing currently and continuously. Jane Roberts' aspect psychology books, *Adventures in Consciousness* and *Psychic Politics,* offer her own experience with Seth's concepts. All of these ideas and more contributed to the learning of Sandy and Sheila during the first few years of their psychic growth. Before their first seminar on reincarnation in January of 1978, they asked Gay for her words on the subject and she offered the following:

> The theory of reincarnation has no rules. All and none of the ideas are correct. Choose one. Work out that, then another. It really does not matter in the end. First is the beginning. It is a circle totally closed. You can neither be inside or outside. You are the circle. You are time, and you are the lives. It is not reincarnation. Only life. Just life. That is all it is. If you wish you could live every life there is.

These words were much less concrete than the various theories they had been reading. How could you live every life there is? As their understanding of the nature of reality grew, they began to experience their oneness and connectedness to all consciousness. Gay's mystical words then began to make sense. By March of 1979, when she spoke the following words to one of Sheila's classes, the awareness of the rich, exciting potential of their individual, but greater selves, was evident to both of them:

> From an overall perspective, you create your influences to learn and to grow in awareness. If nothing influenced you, you would not even be in physical reality. Influences are self created. Lives are self created. You could, if you wish, live every life that exists for you are all one. And these influences are very important. Welcome them and then let go of them when they have served their purpose. Awareness is all. Awareness will help you realize influences and when to let go when it is right for you. There is no past, present, or

future. Your words limit the expression. You think in ways your language reflects. It is difficult to relate because you have chosen physical forms to express concepts of time. It is fine for you, if you wish, to think of past lives. Begin, however, to open to other possibilities. All lives can influence you. It depends on what learning you wish to do. You are all opening psychically, and you will begin to see this in your own ways. Trust your own thoughts. Your ideas are what is reality. Mine are only a perspective and, as a perspective, must be integrated into yours. You must interpret for yourself. You have made a "commitment" to learning, and so I will not tell you everything. You are getting ready to find much for yourselves.

Chapter 9

Visions, etc.

IT WAS A LITTLE after 10 P.M. Sandy had gone to bed with the intention of waking early to do some writing. She read for awhile, turned off the light, and then began to settle into sleep. She had just reached a comfortable, deep pre-sleep state of consciousness and could feel herself rising and floating just a little over her physical body, when suddenly she felt compelled to open her eyes. The room was filled with a light so bright she felt as if day had instantly returned. She thought, "But I've turned out the light — " She looked around the room. Over to her left, floating mid-air in front of her bookcase, she saw a miniature figure — an angel without wings or halo, feminine, cherubic, dressed in white. It was smiling. Sandy's eyes widened in disbelief. The figure then began sending what looked like large balls or rings of fire — brightly colored light — toward her head. The balls pulsated from the figure and entered her head in a steady rhythmic pattern. Frightened, she squeezed her eyes closed and mentally yelled, "Help!" One more ball of light entered her head through her closed eyes; then everything became quiet. Sandy felt wide awake. She opened her eyes and the room was perfectly normal — the only light coming from the nightlight in the bathroom twenty feet away and around the corner. She thought, "I must get up and write this down—" but, before she could move, she fell into a deep, heavy sleep and did not wake up until the alarm went off at 5 A.M.

The next day, while at work, she began working on a story she had started to write a month before and had put aside. That night, November 15, 1977, she and Sheila had a session with Gay. She asked about the "angel" in her bedroom:

Gay: The vision you experienced was energy being sent to help you learn. Often energy is sent, but, of course, many don't actually see this happening to them. It involves a transfer of thoughts to you. You will be hit with some very creative thoughts in the next few weeks. They will seem as if they simply hit you.

Sandy: Why did I see the angel-like person?

Gay: Simply your psyche projecting. It is a force, and from a spiritual level. You do know it is positive, so you saw a positive symbol and white light.

Sandy: Where does it come from? You?

Gay: This was from me and other guides and a couple of writers; two come to mind: Longfellow and Stevenson.

Sandy: Why them?

Gay: They are interested in sending energy to writers.

Sandy: Like Cezanne did to Jane Roberts?[1]

Gay: Not information on themselves. Simple energy to help you write. Very generous men, and wise. You may hear or see them. Remain open to all possibilities.

Sandy: Did the energy I got last night result in my going back to a story I started a month ago?

Gay: Yes, suddenly. It will seem spontaneous, and in one sense it is; but we are sending energy.

Longfellow and Stevenson? Sandy had not read either of these writers sence her childhood. She and Sheila laughed, dismissing the entire incident as fanciful fun. A day or so later, however, Sandy did "hear" from them. She had purchased a stack of paperback books on psychic matters from a used-book store. Waiting for her next appointment for her job, she sat in her car and began to thumb through the books. The first book she picked up, one by Jess Stearn, opened to the center and there on the page was a quote from Longfellow—something about "dust to dust" not applying to the soul. She laughed so hard people walking by her car began to stare at her. Later that same day she stopped to visit a good friend. As they were sitting and talking, Sandy glanced up over her friend's head to a bookshelf, and staring her in the face was Robert Louis Stevenson's *Kidnapped*. The book had been there for years, her friend told her, as it was her husband's favorite childhood book. As many times as Sandy had looked over the books on that shelf, she had never before noticed. Now it jumped out at her.

Looking back over her journals a couple of years later, Sandy realized that she had indeed moved into a creative period. She finished the story that she had been working on, and then three others that will eventually be in a book she has been working on for several years.

---

[1] *The World View of Paul Cezanne*, 1977.

Since the "angel" appeared that November in 1977, Sandy has experienced a half dozen or so similar "visions" in her bedroom – usually just before sleep. Sometimes these floating objects are simply geometric forms. Sometimes they are conventional forms – some familiar, some not. Once she opened her eyes to see, floating mid-air at the foot of her bed, the form of a dog the family had owned but had recently given away. Another time there was the form of a woman. The torso faced toward her but the head was turned to the side with the profile showing. The form faded at the feet and hung in the air. It was dressed in gypsy-like layered clothing and wore a turban-tied scarf on the head. Sandy watched it for several moments before it slowly faded away. After the first experience with the angel, she had ceased to be afraid and simply observed these phenomena. She was aware that these forms were projections of her own mind, the outward physical appearance to energies that surrounded her. She did not let herself become caught by them and, therefore, frightened. Reading in classical spiritualism[1] gave her some explanation for the experiences, as well as Jane Roberts' description of similar "thought projections."[2] Thoughts are real "things," she had learned. They are made up of vibrating energy. Her own consciousness had chosen to create these unusual forms using energy drawn from her own mind and from that sent to her by her guides and higher self. For fun, Gay told her.

These experiences happened to Sandy when her eyes were wide open. She was relaxed and open, but fully awake and alert. The visions, or hallucinations (as the medical profession would prefer to label them), were perceived with her physical eyes. Most of her visions into different realities, however, occur during meditation. These experiences are just as real but are perceived through the inner senses rather than by the eyes. They are a regular occurrence in her meditations and take varying forms. Sometimes they are fleeting glimpses of scenes or objects. One of the early experiences she had, long before she began working with Sheila and Gay, and had given any thought to reincarnation or past lives, was a vivid image of a beautiful, detailed medallion. The image remained with her for several moments and inwardly she heard the words, "5,000 B.C." She felt that this medallion had something to do with her but, at the time, did not have any way to explain the feeling. She often "sees" entire cities in her mind – visionary cities on the horizon, as well as city streets that she feels she is

---

[1] Cf. *Thought-Forms* by Annie Besant and C.S. Leadbeater, (Quest, 1969).
[2] *The Seth Material*, Chapter 14, pp. 194-197.

walking through. Sometimes people appear — often suddenly and vividly, sometimes familiar, sometimes not. Often the visions are symbolic and helpful psychologically in the same way as dreams. On occasion, she has experienced a blending of physical reality with the vision in her mind. Once, not long after she began to meditate regularly, she was sitting in the stuffed, orange chair in her living room, deep in trance, when she "saw" a cup fall off a cabinet. Her physical body reacted to it as if it had actually happened. She started and her hand jumped to catch the cup. She did not "start" because of some outside noise, as often happens when she is deep in trance, but because of the inner event which felt just as real as the actual one of sitting in the orange chair.

Sheila's psychic expriences are not usually visual. They come as strong feelings or thoughts — a "knowing" of something. Occasionally, however, she does experience auditory "hallucinations." One of the most vivid experiences she had, occurred just a few months after first contacting Gay. She had gone skiing with a close friend, Madeline, who had not skiied before and had to rent equipment. The line was long and Sheila was impatient to be on the slopes for the first time that year. She left her friend in the line and went ahead to ski a couple of early runs before the slopes filled. As she rode up the chair lift, she heard her name paged. The voice asked her to return to the desk in the lodge. As soon as she got off the lift and started down the mountain, she heard another page, again urging her to return to the desk. She skiied down quickly and went right to the lodge. There Madeline was waiting. She needed her driver's license from Sheila's locked car in order to rent the skis. "Boy, it's a good thing you paged me or it may have been hours before I came back down."

"Page you? I didn't page you. I did go out looking for you to see if I could stop you before you got on the lift, but I did not page you."

"But, I heard — " Sheila and Madeline began to laugh. They were becoming used to such occurrences in their lives. The incident was more than telepathy, however. That had occurred often between the two friends, but this time Sheila did not just have thoughts or intuitive feelings. She heard, with her physical ears, her name paged on the public address system.

Auditory psychic experiences are not unusual for Sheila. Usually they are auditory glimpses into other realities or "frequencies" that others are not aware of. Often during those first months of talking to Gay, she would suddenly hear different "radio" stations. It was as if her ears were becoming sharper and more attuned than those of others around her. She would be sitting on Sandy's couch, talking to Sandy or Madeline, when suddenly she would ask, "Do you hear the music? It's country music?" Or she would hear a weather report for some distant city like Denver, Colorado. This was so frequent that Sandy and Madeline would laugh and say, "There she goes. Sheila's at it again."

There were two occasions where the music she heard was vivid and sustained and, later, she and Sandy asked Gay about it. The first time was in October, 1977, while she and Sandy were in Scottsdale, Arizona. Sheila was attempting to sleep after a long, tiring day of training, but found herself distracted by the country and rock music coming from the lounge of their resort. Their room was directly across the pool from the lounge and, even with the air conditioner on, the music could be heard in the room. Sheila began to drift into a pre-sleep trance. As she heard the loud popular music coming from the bar, it began to intermingle with the sound of soothing classical music. Before long she heard only the classical music, which eventually soothed her to sleep. The next day she was so struck by the event she had Sandy ask Gay to explain how it could have happened.

> She often visits other realities and places here [Gay's plane of reality] and rather than seeing, hears. She can hear conversations, music and the vibration of atoms and molecules, switching of time, and slipping space. (Was she alseep?) No. She was in between waking and sleeping. The music was from downstairs and then again a concert in 1812 in Vienna.

Almost a year later in August of 1978, Sheila experienced the same kind of phenomena two nights in a row. During a session, she asked Gay where it was coming from.

> The music the first night was symphonies from the city of Prague, and they were going on that evening. The second night was music from Rome. You sometimes listen to far away music.

Sandy, feeling somewhat jealous, asked, "Why not me too?"

> Due to your beliefs about music and your hearing, you see visions instead.

Gay was talking about Sandy's deaf right ear and her fear of music. This was something that she had known and felt all her life. What was interesting here was Gay again pointing out the difference between how the two women perceive psychic phenomena. Sandy "sees." Sheila "hears." As time has gone on, both women have learned to blend both kinds of experience, but it is still more natural for Sandy to see visions and for Sheila to hear other realities. Sheila's auditory messages are often comforting during her work. Sometimes when she is tired or emotionally distracted but has an appointment for a reading, she will "hear" Gay's comforting voice in her right ear, assuring her that she, Gay, is there and everything will go smoothly. It does.

Gay had always stressed that these experiences were natural. After the discussion of Sheila's concerts during that August 1978 session, they asked her why, if psychic experience is so natural, is it so difficult to get in touch with?

Gay: Yes. You have been cut off from the source of energy. It is very natural. The problem is that you really don't see it as natural.

Sandy: Being cut off?

Gay: No. The psychic experiences and other realities. It is natural, life will be easier. You actually think the way you live is natural.

Sandy: It's not?

Gay: No.

Sandy: How did we get cut off from the source?

Gay: It happens as you decide to explore and leave the source, God. You cut yourself off.

Sandy: You mean our journey is back toward God?

Gay: Yes.

Sandy: That's how we learn and grow?

Gay: Yes. Just to learn, basically for fun; but as we cut ourselves off, we did not realize part of cutting off meant forgetting how to enjoy and have pleasure in life.

Sandy: Actually, we are still part of the source?

Gay: Yes. We are the source. You cut yourself off, but you were cutting yourself off from yourself.

Sandy: We're trying to know that again?

Gay: You do know that.

Another mystical explanation! Sandy and Sheila were still learning that the experiences they were having were ultimately to lead them to full knowledge of their connectedness with all life. George Leonard, in his book *The Transformation,* describes such an experience of his own and then speculates on why these experiences are seemingly so rare:

Maybe such moments seem rarer than they really are due to the fact that we have no words for adequately expressing them. One of the more powerful taboo mechanisms is simply not providing a vocabulary for the experience to be tabooed. In this case, you are forced into surrogate vocabularies that can be categorized as mystical or nutty, and easily dismissed; leaving you shamed and doubtful that you really had the experience after all. How many contemporary films, plays, or novels can you bring to mind that deal with unadulterated ecstasy? Positive, unconditional joy may, as a matter of fact, turn out to be the real pornography of these transition years — strange, embarrassing, titillating. (Page 15)

Perhaps the most commonly shared paranormal experience is that of telepathy, especially among people who are close. A woman feels an urgent need to call home to her parents. She does and finds her mother has been hurt in a fall. A child comes home from school and finds his mother at home during a time she's usually working. "Mommy, I knew you would be here long before I saw your car in the driveway." Incidents such as these are so common most people, at one time or another, experience them. Often, however, they are dismissed as coincidences or weird happenings and immediately forgotten.

In her classes, Sheila encourages class participants to pay attention to such incidents and, thereby, learn to trust their own minds and explore the vast potential for communication that exists between people. She uses several exercises to show people how "psychic" they are and how easy it is to pick up other's thoughts. The favorite of most people in her classes is a simple hypnosis technique that hooks two people up at their upper chakra points — the heart, throat, forehead and top of the head. They are then instructed to send "messages" back and forth — usually numbers, colors, animals, geometric shapes, or whatever comes to Sheila's mind. The high incidence of "hits" is usually extremely reinforcing to the class participants.

During a class Sandy happened to attend while this chapter was being written, she had an amusing experience with this exercise. She had linked up with a man with whom she knew she communicated telepathically, so she expected some success with the sending and receiving. As it turned out, she was unable to receive his messages and he received all of hers. That is not unusual, for often one person is a stronger sender and the other a stronger receiver. This varies between people. Sandy and Sheila send and receive to and from each other regularly in their work. The fun part of the exchange during the class came as Sandy and Jonathan were comparing messages. Everything she had sent to him, he had received correctly until they reached the last message. Sheila had instructed them to send an animal. Sandy immediately thought of her cat and began to feel much sadness because the cat was very sick and was expected to die. Under the hypnosis, these feelings were particularly strong, and she was sure that Jonathan would easily pick up this image. However, when they compared notes, he had written "opossum/cat." She looked at him quizzically, wondering how such a miserable animal had gotten in the way of her strong feelings of love and loss for her beloved cat. Then she began to laugh. During the past few weeks she had been having a great deal of difficulty with a huge opossum that had been turning over her garbage cans and strewing trash all over her driveway. She had seen the animal recently one night as she drove in the driveway. Evidently her extreme annoyance at the opossum, though not consciously in her mind at the time of the hypnosis, had been intense enough for Jonathan to pick up on it. He did say that the second image he received after mentally seeing the head of an opossum was that of a cat. Sheila pointed out that it is always important to exchange feedback during incidents of telepathy, for often the messages are not as expected or conventionally predicted.

Sheila and Sandy were speaking to a parapsychology club at a local community college, during the spring of 1980, when Sheila was challenged to a telepathy "contest." In the audience was a young, bouncy, black girl who had contributed to the discussion with many tidbits of amusing information. Her eyes would widen as the two women discussed some part of their work or beliefs; and she would begin enthusiastically nodding her assent, often bubbling over with some story or another about how such a thing had happened to her. She claimed to "always" know what her boyfriend was doing and with whom, much to his distress. Toward the end of the session, she challenged Sheila to a telepathy exchange. Sheila accepted; and the two began to stare intently at each other while the rest of the room remained quiet. After about a minute or so, Sheila began laughing. The girl, excited and jumping up and down in her seat, squealed, "You like me. You are telling me that you like me!"

Sheila nodded and returned, "Yes, and you said the same to me." The girl affirmed that she certainly had. The exchange was simple and yet extremely effective and reinforcing for both of them, as well as the audience.

Much is unknown about the power of such communication, particularly among people who are close. Sandy had an experience that caused her to speculate on the emotional value of telepathic communication. How often do feelings of closeness and caring between people affect the outcome of events through contact on non-conventional levels of relating? Sandy had been dating a successful artist several years older than she. She was feeling quite close to the man and enjoyed being with him. He had gone through several radical life changes just before their relationship had begun, and he was still feeling uncertain about the stability of his new life. One evening, after they had attended a concert, they returned to his apartment for drinks and talk. He began to speak vaguely about his fear of becoming too close to her then hurting her if he went away. At first, Sandy thought this was simply a psychological projection of his fear of being hurt if the relationship did not work out as he wanted. She did not feel that she was unduly dependent upon him for she knew he was still exploring his new-found freedom. She assured him that he need not worry about her feelings. Then the conversation turned to a discussion of different artists who had killed themselves. He named many examples, which Sandy countered with examples of those who had lived full, long lives. Before she left, he showed her a drawing that he had done of himself that she hated. She felt he looked old and sour.

Driving home she began to realize that perhaps he was afraid of dying, and his talk about "going away" or "leaving" had much more to do with his fears than she had originally thought. She decided that she must share with him some words Gay had given her on his creativity and the work he had yet to do.

The next morning she meditated around 10 A.M. She thought of him again and consciously sent him some energy. Then around 10:30 A.M., just toward the end of the meditation, while she was still deep in trance, she began to receive spontaneous images of him as a child. She saw an unhappy child running through a field, then lying crying and hurt while his mother hovered over him. Sandy again sent him love and came out of the trance.

At 12:30 P.M. the phone rang. It was the man. He sounded very upset, telling her that he had had an automobile accident and had just returned from the hospital. He had carelessly run through a red light and crashed into the side of a large Mack truck. His Volkswagon had hit the wheel instead of going under it, where he would have been crushed. The police told him that it was a miracle he was alive. The accident occurred at 10:30 A.M. "And Sandy, the strangest thing! Just as the car was hitting the truck, I saw my mother's face. She died years ago."

Sandy held her breath. All of the implications of the event began to hit her. How many different influences were there to help him through this crucial emotional period and choose life over death? In her small way, she knew that she had made a contribution because she had cared. Evidently the man was cared for from more than one plane of reality.

Consciously leaving the confines of the physical body is one of the most common experiences reported by people who are beginning to develop their psychic selves. Sandy's experiences with such phenomena are described throughout the book. Usually they are spontaneous and without any planning on her part. Often she finds herself somewhere else without conscious memory of "travelling." These experiences are usually triggered by some kind of need or emotional attachment to someone. The experience with her other self described in Chapter 8 certainly occurred because her greater self – or "over soul" – called upon her to aid another part of her being. Another time, just before sleep, she "found" herself with a man she cared for deeply. They were "nowhere" in a physical sense, but his being felt very real and vivid to her. She walked toward him. He put his arms around her, turned her, and lightly kissed the back of her neck. When she realized that this was real and happening and not a dream, she panicked and was again instantly back in her bed. She was sure she had not dreamed the incident and later asked Gay about it. Gay confirmed that the incident had been an out-of-body experience and the emotional closeness she had been feeling with the man during that time had brought about the "meeting."

Another time she was sitting in a chair meditating. She was having difficulty going deeply into trance and had been disturbed about several areas of her life. She wished for the peace of a deep trance and for help to concentrate on affirmations to overcome her difficulties. Suddenly she felt herself being pulled upward. It was as if she were no longer in control of her consciousness but was being "helped" to move onto another level of awareness. She flew out of the top of her head. As she travelled upward, she could see herself in the chair in her living room through the roof of her house. Everything looked small and far away, as if she were looking down from an airplane, but her consciousness felt vast as it telescoped downward to where her physical body sat in the chair in her living room. She was aware of her body, felt connected to it, but also far, far above it. When she reached this high, expanded state of consciousness, she felt the peace that she had sought. Another part of her mind then began to repeat her affirmations and her programming while her conscious mind was quiet and listening. After a time, she contracted and again found herself in the confines of her physical body, sitting in the orange chair in her living room. She felt much better than she had before she began her trance.

That kind of experience is common. Both she and Sheila frequently felt such expanded states of awareness. Having had these spontaneous experiences, Sandy decided to try consciously inducing out-of-the-body explorations. She wanted to astral travel. She read Robert Monroe's *Journeys Out of the Body,* a classic in contemporary psychic literature, which describes his personal, methodical explorations with out-of-the-body travel after he had had a spontaneous experience. Many of the initial, pre-travel conditions that he described, Sandy had felt during her trances: the heaviness of the physical body, the vibrations, the movement around her body, the lifted feeling as if ready for takeoff. For several months, she practiced with little success. She would have all the "symptoms" but, as soon as she was ready, she would become self-conscious and the experiences would end. During that time she had some near misses. Once she could "see" her astral body – or what she thought must be her astral body – do a flip and she was very excited. Often, too, she felt her astral body to be in a different position than her physical body. After awhile she gave up trying to travel consciously out of the body, deciding she must not be ready, and relaxed, allowing the experiences to come as they had before.

Many of Sheila and Sandy's friends have had conscious out-of-the-body experiences, and a few have learned to induce the experience to travel at will. Without awareness of how normal this is, however, the experience can be very scary. Sandy has a good friend who spent many years in prison where he developed his spiritual side and became a serious student of the Islamic religion. Although he read extensively in spiritual areas, he had very little exposure to psychic phenomena; therefore, when he spontaneously started leaving his body during deep meditation, he began to question his sanity. The freedom that this travel gave him, however, was so inviting that he set aside his doubts and continued to explore. He learned how to "leave" at will and travel through different planes of reality. Often he could travel out of the body to "visit" friends and relatives. This ability made his grim prison life somewhat tolerable. He continued to question his sanity, however, and told no one what he was doing. After leaving prison, two coincidences brought his peculiarity out into the open. While visiting a Moslem Mosque, he spent a long period in meditation during which he left his body and travelled about. When he came out of the trance, he looked across the room and noticed a man watching him. He felt as if he had been caught, and indeed he had. The man approached him and told him that he knew what he was doing. He gulped. Then the man went on to describe how he too had learned to travel out-of-body and, after a long discussion, Sandy's friend felt relieved and normal. A few weeks after that, he received in the mail a copy of Monroe's *Journeys Out of the Body* from Sandy, who had thought he might want to learn about this area of psychic experience. She had not consciously known he already had. The book increased his understanding of what was happening and reassured him he was not crazy.

People often ask Gay about out-of-the-body experiences they are either having or trying to induce. One young man received the following from her about his experiences. This is the perspective she usually offers inquiring individuals.

> You leave your body and often visit other places and times. They are very real experiences. Experiences designed to help to clarify events and feelings in the waking state. You can integrate both. You have recently had out-of-the-body experiences. Here I wish to explain what this means. First, the term out-of-body is misleading. Only used because consciousness has usually been limited to the body as if that is its home. The boundaries are set by you. Leaving this self-imposed territory, you are actually expanding your awareness. The consciousness is the whole universe. Everything in your mind belongs there and is a part of you. Leaving the body is really an expansion. You have had what is usually called an out-of-body experience. I gave you this explanation so that you would have another perspective on what is happening to you. (9/20/79)

Sandy and Sheila have not been interested in the area of the occult that conjures up dead relatives or seeks physical manifestation of ghostly presences, such as table rocking, ectoplasmic "appearances" or poltergeist activity. Such phenomena do occur, but their attitude toward such happenings has been, "So what? How is that relevant to me?" They do recognize that, as all reality is mind-created, so is such phenomena; and sometimes for a person's learning — perhaps simply to force attention on greater realities—the creator (that is, the person experiencing this kind of activity) will give himself or herself such an experience. Usually this happens when the person is not trying to induce such experience but during times of intense stress where attention is needed in order to clear the mind to offer new ways of seeing. Just as openness and willingness to experience change and the unknown will bring about transcendent experience, so will the mind work to help a person move into greater awareness by offering unusual or paranormal events. After the paranormal or unusual is effectively integrated into the personality, it becomes a part of life and is no longer experienced as strange. All of life is a beautiful, ever-changing mystery – a vast potential where all is possible. What results then is a closer attention to the self and its magic in its day-to-day living. Everything – each experience, each feeling, each thought – becomes a potential for learning and for expanding the knowledge of who we are and how we are much more than we ever dreamed.

Although Sandy and Sheila do not seek such phenomena, occasionally it happens. One area where physical manifestation of extranormal energies occurred frequently evolved out of a creative project that the women began working on quite unconsciously – communication with "ghosts" or "characters," which is the subject of a book Sandy is writing. These characters began to appear on the Ouija Board shortly after the women started their explorations. A personality other than Gay would make himself or herself known and then insist on relating a story. The women learned that the fastest way to get rid of these characters, so that they could talk to Gay, was to listen to the story. Much later they realized that what was happening involved Sandy's creative potentials, which will be discussed in the next chapter. Pertinent here are the physical disturbances caused by these "characters."

Sandy's former husband had installed a smoke alarm in her house. This particular alarm is powered by a battery and begins to beep repetitively when a fresh one is needed. Sandy's smoke alarm, however, shortly after its installation, began to beep indiscriminately. She cleaned it according to the instructions. The battery was fresh. Nothing seemed wrong with the physical instrument. Soon she began to realize that the beeping occurred while Sheila was there for a private session or a reading, or sometimes if she had been thinking about the characters for her new book. One night during a private sesson, the beeping became insistent and intrusive. They asked Gay what was going on.

"It's George Noble. He wants his presence known." He was one of the characters, and a sort of spokesman, who, cooperating with the energy of the others, beeped to get attention. Sandy and Sheila thought the whole idea was great fun and would simply yell "Hi!" when he beeped and then go back to their business. This form of communication was fine for quite a while, entertaining and not very disturbing. Sandy worked on the stories of the characters as her busy schedule permitted. It was not a major part of her life at that time, but diversion and potential for future creativity.

During February of 1978, she was working on a sketch of one character, named Adam Woxley, whom they had encountered on the Ouija Board the previous year. Halfway through the story, she met a man in whom she became very interested. Her writing stopped for a while as she devoted her energy and time to him. A few months later, during a lull in their relationship, and at a time she was beginning to return to her writing, she and Sheila did a reading for another man. Sandy found him attractive. The smoke alarm beeped. Sheila and Sandy ignored it as they continued the reading. Usually phenomena of this kind did not occur while there were strangers present. Then, toward the end of the reading, there was a crash in the kitchen. A large shadow box filled with beans, rice, and butterflies had fallen and broken into scattered pieces. Sandy was puzzled, as the shadow box had been there several years. In fact, she had recently checked the nails holding it. It had been secure.

They returned to the reading. As Sheila began going into trance, she felt a personality quite different from Gay's. Normally such a thing would never happen during a reading, but because the man was so open and relaxed about the session, Sheila allowed it to occur. The voice that then came through her mouth was definitely masculine and yelled the words, "What about me?" Sheila came out of trance and said she felt it was Adam Woxley. They continued with the reading and, after the man had left, began to realize what had happened. The characters saw that Sandy was apt to be distracted again by another man, and they were jealous. They acted like little children: first buzzing the smoke alarm and, when that didn't work, they (using what must have been an enormous amount of psychic energy) effected the crash of the shadowbox. Sandy felt as if they were trying to run her life and became angry. Play is one thing, but destruction and interruption of a reading were certainly undesirable. She then purposely and ceremoniously took all the pages she had written on the stories, put them in a covered box, and stored them away in the bottom of her desk. Her message to the characters was that she would write the book when she chose. This was her physical reality, and she would create it as she desired. It worked. The smoke alarm stopped ringing. The feeling of swarming presences around the house stopped, and everything was peaceful. Six months or so later, during a private session, Sheila could "feel" the characters around Sandy. She said that they seemed to be saying that they wanted her to know they were still there but did not want to anger her. She laughed and lovingly assured them that she would return to their book. Eventually she did.

The important lesson here is, not only do such energies exist and have the power to make themselves known, but those who draw these energies and experiences to themselves for whatever purpose — creativity, learning, resolution of grief, or unfinished business with a dead relative, or whatever — are in control. They are creating their own lives, as we all do at any time; and awareness of this is important. It is often easy for someone who fears the unknown to give away their personal power and allow such energy to run their lives. The person in physical reality has total control of that reality and the right to say "no" to anyone — whether it be another physical person or a non-physical entity.

The other area where dealing with extra-normal energies resulted in physical manifestation of unusual phenomena is less colorful, but quite interesting. After Gay began speaking through Sheila, Sandy began taking down her words in shorthand. She had learned shorthand twenty years earlier but had never used it and assumed that she had forgotten most of it. As Gay talked, it began to return and became the method they found most comfortable for recording the messages. Occasionally they would suggest using a tape recorder, but Gay would say no, that she preferred the method they were using. She insisted she liked Sandy's involvement and that Sandy contributed needed energy. The women, therefore, made no conscious attempt to record the sessions. They found that they preferred having the material written in space, rather than recorded in time. It was more accessible and durable. They knew tapes could be untrustworthy, sometimes not work, and could be too easily destroyed. They accidentally discovered, however, that they would have been unsuccessful.

They were to do a reading for an old friend from their therapy group. Before the woman arrived, they hooked their tape-recorders together with a patch cord in order to make a copy of a hypnosis tape that Sheila had wished to give to a friend. This was a procedure they had successfully used many times. The next day Sheila sent the copied tape to her friend. A day or so later, the friend returned the tape saying that, rather than the expected hypnosis session, the tape played what sounded like a private conversation. She did not feel she should listen, so she was returning it. Puzzled, Sheila put the cassette in her recorder and found that the tape had recorded the conversation that had occurred between herself, Sandy, and the woman who had come for a reading. She had evidently botched the hookup between the recorders, so the session itself had been recorded. "Good," she thought, "I'll finally be able to hear what Gay sounds like." She had to take others' words as to how she sounded during trance and how differently Gay talked from the way she did. She listened through the preliminary conversation, heard herself lie down on the couch and ask for Gay. She heard her deep breathing as she went into trance, and then – nothing. The tape was empty from that point on. The entire session should have been taped, for she had let the recorder run to the end of the tape before turning it over to record the other side. When they asked Gay about it, she simply told them again that she did not like tape recorders and preferred the shorthand method.

At a later time, however, she did make an exception. When David Palladin was in the East in May of 1978, doing a seminar for the women, all of his "spooks" talked to the seminar participants. David always records his sessions. Many there were taping Kandinsky, Gottlieb and others, who talked to the group through David. At one point in the seminar, Kandinsky invited Gay to say a few words in exchange with him. Sheila went into trance – for the first time in front of a large group of people – and Gay spoke. Later, when they listened to the tape, her voice was recorded and Sheila heard her for the first time. Other attempts during the sessions and at classes, however, have been unsuccessful.

During the summer of 1979, a young woman came to a session with the parents of a friend who had died. She had heard Sheila and Sandy speak to a parapsychology class and felt that Gay could help all of them understand the girl's untimely death and subsequent communication through dreams and "coincidences." When they arrived, the young woman had a tape recorder. She announced that she knew Sandy and Sheila had told the class that Gay did not like to be recorded, but she really wanted to try. Her tape recorder was an expensive dictating model. She had tested it before she arrived, and it worked fine. Sandy shrugged and said okay. They put the recorder near Sheila's head, as she lay on the couch. Sandy picked up her notebook and took down the first trance. Excited, the girl reached for the recorder, anxious to hear how well the session taped. The tape was jammed. Nothing had been recorded. When the session ended, the young woman and older couple went outside to their parked cars.

They stood and talked for a while. Sheila and Sandy still had business to discuss, but Sheila went to her car for something she had forgotten. She found the three of them very excited. They had decided to try the recorder again to see if it worked. It did. Perfectly.

Perhaps Gay, like us all, wants to create her reality in the manner that she desires.

Chapter 10

Creativity

SHEILA WAS DRIVING DOWN River Road, when her car stopped. She looked at her gas gauge; a quarter tank to go. "What am I going to do?" she thought. She was far from town. There were a few houses scattered along the road, but no gas stations for several miles. Sheila had owned the car about a week. She had totalled her reliable and familiar Datsun, just a week or so before in an accident on the winter ice. A friend sold her his old Opel for a modest price. This car still felt strange to her. She had yet to learn its peculiarities. As she sat there, she decided to call on Gay. "Perhaps she can help," Sheila thought. She settled into her seat, began breathing regularly and moved into trance. "Okay, Gay. What's wrong with this car?"

"Nothing."

Nothing...but the car won't start. Sheila tried again, but it still wouldn't start. She asked Gay again.

"Nothing."

Frustrated, Sheila tried starting the car again. It would not start. "Something is wrong with this car! What does Gay know about cars anyway?" she angrily thought. "I'll ask the spirit of the car." She settled into trance again, concentrating on calling up the "spirit" or "consciousness" of the car. "Okay, car, what is wrong with you."

"Nothing." It came through loud and clear this time. The answer was always the same. Sheila was very frustrated. She sat there for a while, a thought teasing the back of her mind. "Perhaps this car is out of gas. 'Nothing' *may* be wrong." She left the car and called a friend. He came with some gasoline. The car started immediately. Nothing was wrong with it. She had been asking the wrong question, but the communication was valid.

Sheila's romance with the old green Opel lasted about a year and a half. During that time, she was to learn a great deal about her own unique kind of creativity. The old green car was very tired. Often it would not, or could not, start. Sheila learned to approach the car very lovingly. When it resisted moving, she would close her eyes and mentally concentrate on sending the car energy. "The entire universe runs on energy," she thought. "My little car can certainly use energy in whatever form it is given." It usually worked. Sometimes it took a little longer than at others, and once it took the combined energies of both Sheila and Sandy.

There was four feet of snow on the ground. The temperature hovered around 10°F. Sandy's long driveway was not plowed. She had shovelled enough space to park two cars, one behind the other. Sheila had come to do a couple of readings, and had parked directly behind Sandy's company car. When she left to go home about 11 P.M., her car would not start. No amount of concentrating seemed to perk it up. She spent the night at Sandy's. The next morning, she tried again. No luck It was nearing time for Sandy to leave for work. She had an early appointment and had to get started. Both women sat down and mentally concentrated on Sheila's car, projecting streams of warm energy into the engine. The car started, and Sandy reached her appointment on time.

Sheila's confidence was pretty high later that year when she went out to her garage to start her car. "Okay, car. You'd like a little energy, would you?" Sheila relaxed and mentally sent the engine streams of energy. Nothing. She tried again. Again nothing. This time she asked the right question. "Car, I've sent you energy. Why won't you start?"

As Sheila listened, she mentally "heard" the words come back. "My brakes are bad. It's too dangerous for you to be out on the road with me. I will start the day you take me to the mechanic."

That was on a Sunday afternoon. Monday morning Sheila made an appointment with the mechanic for Thursday. Each day until Thursday, she tried to start the car. She could not. On Thursday morning, she began "talking" to the car in her mind. She said over and over that this was the day it was to have its brakes fixed. When she went out to drive to the mechanic, the car started immediately. After the brakes were fixed, Sheila never had another problem with the engine.

At the same time Sheila was learning about communication with automobiles, she was given Gus. Gus was a cute little brown-striped kitten, with a smattering of white. He was full of energy. Soon it became apparent that his energy was so abundant and his behavior subsequently so obnoxious that Sheila was about to lose all of her friends. Anytime anyone entered her apartment, Gus would bound out from wherever he had been gleefully destroying something and in a running jump, would attack whoever entered, digging his well sharpened claws through dresses, shirts, sweaters, even coats. He thought this was great fun. Sheila's friends did not. Sheila realized she would have to do something; either her cat or her friends would have to go. She decided to try hypnotizing the cat. A couple of times a day, for several days, she would seduce the cat into her lap or on to the couch next to her. There she would pet him lightly, talking an hynpotic patter. Gus would seemingly go to sleep. Sheila would continue talking softly, giving him suggestions on his behavior. Then she would count him up as if he were a client and she was doing a regular hypnosis session. He always woke up on the count of five! She was sure then that was similar to a hypnotic trance, rather than a natural sleep. The proof that it was working, however, was in his behavior. Within a week, he had calmed down considerably. Friends found they no longer had to duck as they walked in the door. Gus continued to be a frisky kitten, and later, an energetic cat...but he was no longer obnoxious and unruly.

Sheila was learning that to be a medium was to engage in a very creative kind of communication. She slowly and sometimes painfully learned about her own creativity. A delightfully creative man named Itzhak Bentov wrote a wonderful book in which he pushes our conventional ideas about the nature of physical reality far beyond their limits, to a new and exciting possibilities. In that book, *Stalking the Wild Pendulum,* he wrote:

> My basic premise is that consciousness resides in matter; put another way, all mass (matter) contains consciousness (or life) to a greater or lesser extent. It may be refined or primitive. We human beings are so designed that when properly trained, we can interact with anything that has consciousness on whatever level. (Pages 96-97)

Part of Sheila's learning included listening to her own body. That listening also taught her more about her own creative process. There had been times during the past three or four years that she had written poetry and written frequently in her journal about her thoughts and feelings. She enjoyed this and felt creative while she was doing it. Then she became busy with her job and with Mind Matters. Time for the writing did not seem to be there. She began to feel barren and empty. The feelings began to manifest themselves physically through pain in her sexual organs. She had recurring pelvic infections and often the pain was severe. She began to talk to her body. She needed direction and understanding of what was happening to her. Sheila did all that she knew to do physically. She improved her diet, took the right vitamins, visited doctors, had chiropractic adjustments, and sent her body healing energy. All of the techniques helped to heal her, but discovering the psychic nature of her pain was important. One day she sat at her typewriter and asked her body to explain her problem—what she needed to know about herself. The answer was an essay on her kind of creativity.

> The pain is a manifestation of your frustration at what you think is buried creativity. Sexual organs are a part of regeneration and life/creativity. A change in the outlook toward your work is necessary now. The readings must be seen by you for the valuable aid they are to others. The pain is not so much sexual guilt, but the denial of your own worth and beauty. Take such times as this to sit and write or type thoughts to the self. You are a creative person. Mind Matters is a beautiful creation. Value who you are and what it is you do....Life is creativity, and if you deny your own ability to create, you deny the life inside of you. It is only natural that it would manifest in this particular area of your body now. Guilt at doing nothing. That is what has been happening to you. In truth, you do much, but it will never be enough for you with your present thoughts. To be is enough. To be is all there is. To be is beauty and truth. To be is love. To be is peace and harmony. To allow this is to be restored to wholeness. (5/22/80)

It is in just being that Sheila creates. She was discovering that her life was her creation. By being still, she could allow a special kind of communication to occur through her that brings valuable insight and wisdom to many. She had always compared herself with others, believing that she lacked because she did not produce a product — a poem, some music, a painting. She was discovering a different kind of art. She may write or paint, but when she does it will be for the personal joy of expressing who she is.

In the Fall of 1978, Sandy and Sheila sent out a mailing asking if anyone was interested in a creative writing class. Sandy had agreed that she could teach such a class if there were interested people. She had taught English a long time before and could see the possibility of combining some of the techniques she had been learning with this background to create a new kind of writing class. She did not expect a response, however, and had agreed to put it in the Mind Matters bulletin to quiet Sheila's urgings. They had also put in a series of classes on reincarnation with weekly group regressions, and she was quite sure that the series would fill, as people were always interested in exploring past lives. She was quite surprised. Before the week was out, seven people had signed up for the writing class. No one had even called about the regressions. This threw Sandy into a quandry. All of her doubts about her abilities began to rise up and flood her consciousness with fear. Sheila couldn't understand her reluctance. "Of course you can do it. What have you been preparing for?"

"Sheila, I don't know if I can even write myself, much less teach others. All I have are a few attempts at some short stories and my journals. What right have I to think I can teach creative writing?"

Her frustration was strong. She did not believe that she was creative, even though she had been learning for some time now that she was and proved it daily. Sheila laughed and said, "Now you know how I feel when I'm afraid a reading isn't going to work!"

This often had been the situation. Sandy could clearly see that Sheila had talent and great creative potential to fulfill and often encouraged her when she was feeling doubtful. Sometimes she felt jealous because Sheila's talent was so obvious and immediate, whereas all she ever did was "take the notes." Of course, her reason knew better. She did make a significant contribution to the sessions with clients, often helping them to interpret Gay's material and ask the correct questions, but she still felt like a secretary. Sheila, on the other hand, had similar feelings. She would sometimes believe that what she was doing was intangible, worthless — that all she was was a channel for words coming from somewhere else that had nothing to do with her. "Just a sieve!" she would complain. "You're going to write a book. That's real. Writing is creative. You're the lucky one."

These doubts swung back and forth between the women during their beginning years, as they each learned of their potential and their own unique creativity. On the day before Sandy's creative writing class was to begin, Gay had the following to say to her about the new class and her relationship with Sheila:

> You are frightened of your own abilities. Trust that you are not being asked to do anything beyond you at all. It is becoming time to believe in yourself. You have 'asked' for these abilities, both the psychic and the writing. When you write, ask, before you start, to be a channel for love, and then begin. There has been a purpose for your involvement with the psychic world and with Sheila. You must trust each other's judgment, for within each of you is much, and you can bring out the best in each other. You look at each

other and see talent and ability. Doubts you express to each other
are reflections of each other. Every time you encourage each other,
you are actually encouraging yourself. There is no one 'star' in this
production. Each of you is developing at about the same rate. As
the weeks go by, you will look back and wonder about this fear.
There was a reason that Thursdays turned to writing instead of
past-life class. You are a good hypnotist, but writing is a love that
cannot be denied. This is where your heart really is. Write from
your heart, and put away the fear of being judged. Work done
with love is always beautiful. I love you and would not direct you
on a wrong path. (10/5/78)

    September 27, 1976. Sheila, Sandy and Madeline had recently
begun their relationship with Gay Bonner. Sheila was very excited. She
was beginning to realize her ability to "receive" direct communication
from Gay. She was trusting her thoughts, high on their new adventure
into a new perspective. She and Madeline had attended a seminar
during the weekend on consciousness raising techniques and
metaphysical theory. They sailed into Sandy's house on Sunday night
for their scheduled session on the Ouija Board with Gay. Bubbling with
enthusiasm from their weekend activities, they excitedly told Sandy
that they had made contact with Gay during the seminar. Sheila
received bits of automatic writing while sitting in a relaxed, altered
state of consciousness. These "messages" were little blurbs on potential creative directions for several of Sheila's friends. Sandy was one of
them. "Look," Sheila cried. "Here's yours!"
    Sandy took the piece of yellow paper. As she read it, she turned
white. "What's the matter?" Madeline asked. "Isn't that okay?"
    Sandy felt as if one of her deepest secrets had been revealed. The
paper read:

> Message from Gay for Sandy Winney. Her work to be done.
> Expression through books. No, not reading. Ability to write. A
> novel in her. Maybe more than one.

    Sandy had always wanted to write. In fact, she had always
written but never openly for others to read. She kept journals. She
wrote letters — most never mailed. She wrote stories occasionally —
usually to express some pent-up feelings or communicate her perceptions of a situation to someone close to her. During her college career,
she had written much as an English major, and her teachers had often
given her encouragement and support. She would usually dismiss this,
saying they were being "nice"; or she would not hear the positive

remarks, tuning in totally on the little things they would find wrong. If anyone would ask her whether or not she, as an English major, had ever thought of writing, she would answer that she had no imagination. She was okay on doing synthesis work – the criticism and journalistic papers she did as an undergraduate and even later in graduate school, but "real" writing – no. She did not have the drive or talent. So she had always believed. She did become interested in helping others write books during her post-graduate years, but the situations never fully materialized, and so her writing had remained a secret. Now Sheila, who consciously knew nothing of this aspect of Sandy's life, was telling her she had an ability to write, and that this was to be her "work." Her fear was so evident that Sheila and Madeline urged her to ask Gay about it. Gay told her that there was some childhood incident that she would remember when she was ready, which would explain some of it.

During the next few weeks, with the help of her therapy group and meditations, she did become in touch with much of what had created her fears. She had begun writing very early – as early as the third or fourth grade – but for a number of psychological reasons, had come to believe that she could not write because she had no imagination or talent. She grew up believing that she was intelligent because she could get good marks in school. In fact, good marks were required, but to express herself fully in a creative or imaginative way was forbidden. She began to discover these deep personal beliefs about herself and let go of them. The process took her several years but, as she explored her beliefs and the influences reinforcing them, she began to write. Along the way, she found beliefs about lack of talent; not deserving to be successful or *do* what she enjoyed for a living; not having enough time to be creative; not being able to enjoy a close, intimate relationship with a man and be creative at the same time; a fear that if she let others know what she could do, they would not like her, and so on. During this process, around the time she was beginning the creative writing classes, Gay pulled some of it together for her. She also raised the question of the responsibility to return creative energies asked for back to the earth:

> You have a deep fear of success. That is all that is in your way. Deep inside of you there is a knowing of truth, and the truth is you are very talented and can do much, but you fear reactions of others. You do not want anyone to think that you are better than they are, for this means you may lose their love. You deserve to be

successful – not only that, but since you have asked for higher energies, there is a responsibility to use these energies to give to the earth which you are part of. Much has been given you. You are loved very much, and I want you to know this. Love from here and many people, too. You can indeed be successful and maintain simplicity and joy. Success does not mean you will be controlled by others. (That's my fear?) You need to hear this now. (It makes me want to cry –) That is why I say this to you. Do not be ashamed to be loved. Do not be ashamed to take of the earth, and do not be ashamed to take credit for all you do. You have a physical existence which will always include an ego, and this is not bad. Be proud of your skills and talents. Rejoice. Help others rejoice in theirs also. (October 1978)

Sandy learned a lot from her creative writing class. Originally scheduled for six weeks, the class was extended to four months. During that time, Sandy pulled together her own methods for exploring creative potential, in order to share them with the class members. This, and the different experiences offered by the others, helped her to see objectively the changes that had been occurring in her life. The creative process in the classes took several directions. The technical aspects of writing were the most practical and least exciting for her. For that, she drew upon her college and teaching background. She also explored beliefs concerning creativity with the class – cultural and personal beliefs. This was an ongoing process as they explored their thoughts and feelings through their writing experiences. They would then develop affirmations to program new thoughts in their minds to replace the old, limiting ones. For Sandy, the most exciting part of the class was the use of trance states, or altered states of consciousness, to find and develop creative writing material. Just as Sheila was using hynposis in her guide-contact classes to open her class members to their psychic potentials, Sandy used similar techniques to help class members discover the deep wells of imagination and creativity available to them for potential expression. She had discovered this herself quite accidentally during the summer of 1977.

While Sandy and Sheila were still working with the Ouija Board, they occasionally would contact personalities other than Gay Bonner, who were usually angry and insistant. These characters always seemed to have a story to tell, and the women found that if they listened, they would have their say and leave the board so that Gay could come through. Gay's only comment had been to enjoy the stories and not take them too seriously. Often the characters would ask the women to tell them what to do or demand that the women do something outrageous on their behalf. One man, who had been hung by the Ku Klux Klan in Alabama in the 1920s, wanted Sheila and Sandy to go there and avenge him, as some of his murderers were still alive. Others would complain bitterly that they had been wronged and would ask for advice on how they could get even with those who had killed or betrayed them. Sandy and Sheila found them either amusing or annoying, depending on their mood and how quickly they wanted to speak to Gay.

It had not occurred to them that there would be any purpose in the appearance of these characters, until July of 1977, when they were attending Sutphen's seminar in Scottsdale. That week was very stimulating and creative for both women. Much time was spent exploring the vastness of their individual consciousnesses. Many of the usual limits were removed, or at least pushed out, so that they had more room in which to play and explore. New ideas and concepts came at them daily, and the potential for expansion and creativity seemed endless.

On Friday morning, five days into the seminar, Sandy attended an early meditation. As she followed the guided instructions of the group's leaders, she mentally asked for direction in her writing. When she was deeply in trance, she began to "see" a parade of characters walking through her mind's visual field. She passively watched, as they floated by. Then the word "sketches" came into her mind. That was all, and she did not know what it meant. During the remainder of that day, however, she felt a kind of mental pressure, as if something inside of her wanted desperately to be heard. That evening she decided to skip the lecture and stay in the room by herself, to see if anything could come through. She went into trance and picked up her pen. She did not have to wait long. First she received some automatic writing from Gay, giving her some practical advice about using spiritual protection and trusting the flow to come through her. A new spirit wished to communicate and would use her trance and her pen. She mentally asked, "Who are you?" and the words began to flow:

> Noomahn. I want to talk to you. I am an Indian. I will tell you my story, and you can tell it for me.

He and five of his Indian companions were betrayed and killed during the 19th century in a Colorado hotel fire that had been deliberately set. They were there trying to negotiate for Indian rights. After he finished the story, he said:

You can write about this. It is in you. You do not believe it yet, but open your mind to the possibility, and you will get a sketch. The knowledge and message is there. You do not have to worry about now knowing. It is all there in you. Just open and let it flow. Many spirits have stories to tell, and they will come to you so that you can tell them. Don't worry about tying them together. That's all done in you already — it will be apparent. Call them spirit stories — 'sketches'. They will be about dying and wanting their stories told. They will sometimes try to cajole you into things you do not want to do, but you can say no. Just write their stories. Go to them by altering your consciousness as you did tonight, and the ideas and stories will come.

Then the writing finished, but Sandy remained in trance. She began to receive images of the story she had just channeled. She witnessed the events of the story in her mind in full color, experiencing the fire, the deaths, and even the movement toward the spiritual plane. Just as she finished the trance and counted herself up, Sheila returned from the evening lecture. They were both excited about the potential of "Sketches."

The writing of these stories is a joint creative effort. Sheila's part in the project became apparent the next morning. She began speaking for Gay regularly that week, so they put the Ouija Board aside. During lunch hour on Saturday, the day after Sandy's trance work, the women decided to speak to Gay about something that had happened during the morning session. As Sheila began to go deeply into trance, Sandy noticed that something unusual was happening. Sheila's features were distorted and her mouth began to move in an exaggerated and twisted manner. Before Sandy had a chance to ask what was happening, a distinctly masculine, very loud voice came spitting out of her friend's mouth:

"Do NOT block me. Don't get in my way."

"Who are you?"

"ROOS"

"Where are you from?"

"Ahman"

"Why are you here?"

"To help. Don't get in my way."

"But why are you here?"

"To say what I have to say. I want to be in 'Sketches'. You will listen to me. I want to say that I was in 5220 long ago in Ahman. They sent me out in exile — not fair."

Sheila came out of trance laughing. During their session with Gay, she gave them more information on Roos. Evidently Ahman was located where the Sahara Desert is today. Roos was exiled but, according to Gay, was very much responsible for his own fate. She explained to Sandy that there would be more characters of this sort, and that she and Sheila could have a lot of fun with them. Since that time, there have been about fifteen to appear. Sometimes they would speak through Sheila. Sometimes they would appear in Sandy's meditations. They even met one in physical life who had all the characteristics of his spirit counterparts. Sandy did find that she could go into trance, ask for one of them by concentrating on the name they had given, and then receive additional material on their stories and psychological makeup. They are exaggerations of all of us, and every one has taught the women something about the foolishness of remaining stuck in emotional states of mind.

It was these experiences that Sandy used as a starting point in her creative writing class; guiding the class members through trance states, as she offered varying suggestions for exploration. Sometimes she would suggest that they concentrate on a photograph or a newspaper article. Other times they would explore their past lives, or other inner realms of their minds. The result was satisfying, and most participants in the class received material for creative use. Most important to Sandy was how much the class gave her in return for her efforts. As she could see their creative ideas unfold, she was inspired to explore her own. Many of her limiting beliefs about having no imagination floated away.

Many of the readings are concerned with an individual's creative potentials. Gay will usually describe past-life influences that can be exploited to develop a person's creative powers, suggesting that one expand creative endeavors currently being pursued, or that one develop new talents not yet explored. Most people have many directions they can explore, but occasionally the intensity of one direction surprises them. One young woman who came to talk to Gay was told that she had more musical talent than she had previously thought. She could, Gay said, use that talent to develop music therapy for emotionally disturbed or retarded people. Two days later, upon arriving at work, she found a pile of journals on her desk describing that kind of work. She never found out where they came from.

Another woman was told that she had writing abilities. She vehemently denied it, insisting that she "hated" writing of any kind. This was one of the earliest readings, and Sheila and Sandy had not yet learned to trust the material fully. They also still felt that they had to please everyone who came. They kept going back to Gay over and over, trying for another direction that would please the woman. Gay was insistent, and the answer was always the same: writing. The woman left so unsatisfied that they did not expect to hear from her again. They did not. However, a couple of years later, Sandy ran into her husband, who told her that the woman had decided to go back to school. She took a primary re-entry course at a local college which required weekly an amount of writing. She complained but wanted to be admitted to school, so she wrote. Her very first paper was highly praised by the teacher. Before the end of the term, she was writing voraciously and loving it!

Being alive is being creative. This message has come through repeatedly from Gay in the readings Sheila and Sandy have done over the years. Sheila learned that her very being was her creativity...the specialness of her consciousness and the beauty that she could allow to flow through her out into the world.

During a raging snowstorm in the winter of 1979, Sandy sat alone in her bedroom, raging with her own emotional storm that she wanted very much to put into a poem. She asked Gay for help and received a page of writing which ended with some words on creative effort:

> Let happen now the poetry in you, and write. You can write as you want and shape the waves, the feelings, the storm, into expression for YOURSELF. You always write for yourself and not others, and then it is good. Go into trance and sit with a pen and let the words flow through you. That is the secret – to you it is still a secret – of the universe and life, as it is the secret to art in your world. It comes from the source of all things and happens when you allow it to – not when you try to make it happen. Knowing that makes it possible to never lose it and to just flow and love. (2/19/79)

Chapter 11

Staying Grounded
INTERPRETING PSYCHIC INPUT

SHEILA AND SANDY HAD met the young man now sitting in the back seat of Sandy's car a few months earlier during a trip they had taken to New York City. He was a practicing psychic who had been excited about the possibility of exchanging some work with them. He was also the first psychic they had met personally since they had begun doing their work a year and a half before. Neither had ever had their cards read, their palms read, their handwriting analyzed, their futures predicted, their astrological charts done, nor experienced any of the various offerings coming from the psychic supermarket. So they, too, were pleased that Frank had agreed to travel from the city to Bucks County in order to meet with them. They had liked his openness and sincerity when they had met before. As they talked now, they learned that he had come from a family of psychics, and so had been raised with a natural acceptance of his talent and special kind of seeing. He was currently doing palm readings and, most frequently, practiced his art at parties and club meetings, where he was hired as an entertainer. His readings, they gathered, were quick and fun for the participants, although he assured them that he always "told what he saw." He and Sheila began talking about their mutual experiences with various clients, and their feelings about doing readings. He seemed somewhat naive about what it was he did and was quite simple in his beliefs and concepts about metaphysics and psychology. He had done very little reading in either area, but Sandy felt him to be honest and likeable. As they rode in the car, he began giving them his impressions — especially those he had of Sheila and her involvement in psychic work. When they arrived at Sandy's house, he did a long reading for Sheila, which mostly centered on her work and personal characteristics, such as her warmth and spontaneity in dealing with people. He was accurate and positive in his approach to her. She was very pleased with his perform-ance. He did make a lot of predictions about money and marriage that seemed dubious, but the women felt this was fun and did not take it seriously.

Next, Frank read the palms of Sandy's sons, Steven and Griffin. He was fairly accurate on their different personality traits, but some-times seemed to confuse the boys, attributing to one the characteristics of the other. On occasion, that had happened during sessions with Gay whenever someone's children were discussed. The women understood that, because Sandy's children are very close emotionally and men-tally, it was quite normal for the mix-up. He again made predictions, however, as to how they would "make money" and relate much later in life to each other and the world. Again, the women could under-stand that he was projecting a future based on their way of being in the world as it is now. Then he began insisting that Steven was going to catch a cold or get sick in the near future. Sandy jumped in immedi-ately and stopped him. She explained that Steven was highly suggesti-ble and that if indeed that probability did lie in Steven's future, she would rather Steve be told to concentrate on seeing himself well and happy rather than be warned that he was going to get a cold. She was thinking to herself that no one needed to hear such predictions, espe-cially her sensitive older son. She was much too aware of the power of suggestion and the tendency of most human beings to actualize a potential future if they are told by someone in authority that some-thing "was going to happen." Frank was serious about his predictions and projected them as fact and inevitable. Rather than present his material with the qualifying "I feel..." or "It seems to me..." that Gay always used when talking to someone, he presented everything he picked up during his readings with "You are...", "It is..." or "It will ..." He was very definite about what he was "seeing."

Now it was Sandy's turn to be "read." Sheila had been feeling very good about her life and herself during the time of this meeting. Steven and Griffin were their usual happy selves. However Sandy, at this particular point in her life, was experiencing a great deal of emo-tional turmoil and much inner pain. Her younger sister had died unex-pectedly and mysteriously just two weeks before. She was also going through a major upheaval in a relationship that was very important to her. She was depressed, crying much of the time, and very confused about herself and her ways of relating to others and the world. Frank picked up these feelings immediately. He told her that she needed to be held so that she could cry and cry. That was certainly true. He then began to tell her that she was a person "who always trusts the wrong people, who were always letting her down." She always expected people to do certain things that they did not do, and they always hurt her. "You don't need people like that around you and should let go of them," he insisted. This seemed to be all that he could pick up around her. Whenever she asked about something else in her life, he would return to the same thing. He did pick up that she was working as a nurse, or in some kind of medical area. That, of course, related to her pharmaceutical sales job, but other than that, all he could see was an overwhelming need to cry and let go of untrustworthy people.

Sandy began to feel very angry and frustrated. She understood that he was accurately picking up her feelings of sadness and depression. The material about being let down by others in life could also be explained by her sister's death, as well as some recent events that had occurred in her relationships. She felt very defensive, however, about his implication that she "always trusted the wrong people." She had worked very hard in her therapy and her recent psychic work to let go of having expectations about other people's behavior. She felt as if she had made progress with this part of her personality. She did recognize that her expectations frequently had set her up to be hurt in the past, but she had come to realize that it was not others who "let her down" but her own unrealistic ideas of how people should or should not behave. As she sat there fuming about what he was saying, she began to realize that she felt as if he thought that what he said she was, was the way she always was—as if she were somehow defined by his description of how she felt at this particular moment in time. His choice of words had made her feel as if she would never be different than what she was at this particular time in her life. As she began to realize where her anger was coming from, and as she put it all into perspective, she felt better and was able to open again and relate to him.

Frank then had his turn; and as Gay talked to him about his relationships, Sandy began to realize that many of the feelings she had had during her reading belonged to him. He felt betrayed by many people in his life. He did not feel he would be loved for himself alone, but only if he took care of others. People were always letting him down. His feeling was that he could cry and cry. He also felt that there was nothing that could be done about the situation. He was stuck. What had happened earlier was now obvious. He had tapped into Sandy's current state of unhappiness, and because it was so closely aligned with his own personal beliefs and deepest feelings, he began projecting his own situation onto her. He was unable to see beyond

Sandy's immediate state of mind to other, more lasting parts of her personality because those same feelings were fixed in him. Believing that that was the way life really was, he saw her as set and totally defined by her temporary feelings. Sandy resented being told that she had to be a certain way and that nothing could be done about it. She knew her situation was temporary, her feelings fluid, and her beliefs changing as she learned and grew. Sheila and Sandy then urged Frank to let go of his limiting beliefs and to open to the possibility that he could enjoy unconditional love and personal power over the direction of his life.

In their work, Sheila and Sandy sometimes find that they are doing what they have come to refer to as "repair work." In several areas of their psychic experience and work, they or others sometimes lose their perspective and become, as it were, ungrounded or imbalanced in regard to a particular situation. Someone will call who has recently seen another psychic, upset and scared about what was said. The person may feel "defined" or "fixed" by a situation or certain personality traits that a particular psychic has picked up on. One young woman, a friend of Sheila's, had visited a psychic while at home in Virginia. The psychic was highly recommended, and Sheila's friend, Gigi, wanted additional confirmation and direction about some psychic work she had begun recently. Sheila had been encouraging her to develop her trance abilities so that she could eventually do psychic work similar to Sheila's. She had a natural talent, and her work was proving to be positive and accurate for the people around her. Both Sandy and Sheila experienced helpful sessions with her and felt that she would have much to offer as a psychic counselor.

At the time that she went to the psychic in Virginia, she had some health problems but felt she was taking positive steps to correct them. She wanted to ask about her work, as well as some questions about her family. As she walked into the office, the psychic looked at her with horror and stated, "There is nothing good in your aura!" She then went on to build the entire reading around Gigi's health and how bad it was. Everything in her life, according to the psychic, depended upon her "getting her health together." Her relationship with her lover, her work, everything predicted for her immediate future was predicated on this. She heard statements like, "Your relationship is good, if you would only get your health in good shape." "Trance work is a lousy idea for you — you are not in good physical health." Gigi's health was a concern. That was accurate. However, related to her health were factors concerning her relationship with her lover and her feelings of being pressured into doing the trance work for others. None of these feelings were mentioned. The entire emphasis was on physical health. The implication was that she, and she alone, must immediately correct the imperfections discussed or her relationship and her potential psychic work were worthless and impossible. She left feeling inadequate and depressed. She hid, refusing to see any of her friends who may have been able to give her some positive encouragement and feedback. She felt that so much was wrong with her, no one would want to be around her. It was three weeks before she finally consulted Sheila and agreed to talk to Gay. Since the psychic had emphasized her "sick" aura, Sheila felt some additional help might be in order. She called Sandy and asked if Sandy's twelve-year-old, Steven, could help.

Steven has a natural ability to see auras—the colors around our physical bodies which indicate the amount and quality of the energy around us. Many psychics work with auras. They learn to interpret what the different colors mean in terms of emotional states and physical health. Since Steven had always seen these colors, he had assumed that everyone experienced them and never said anything about it. Sandy discovered his ability accidentally. Fascinated, she often questioned him about the different colors he saw and what they meant to him. For instance, Steven had told her that he could always tell when she was feeling angry, as a dark, deep red would appear around her head. Most of the time though, he was aware only of the various colors he could see and the extent to which the aura had expanded out from a person's body. To him, some people had big auras and some had little auras. The colors were pretty and varied from person to person and changed constantly. He had not yet developed any concepts about how these color changes correlated to moods. He did notice, however, that when someone was sick or not feeling good, his or her aura became smaller and darker. Sheila felt that his innocence and ingenuous nature would help Gigi put her experience into perspective.

When Gigi and Sheila arrived, Sandy asked Steven to describe the colors around each of them, and also to show them how far the colors extended. He reported that Gigi had much orange around her body, with purple on the outside. He said the colors were clear and pretty. They extended a good five feet out in every direction from Gigi's body. Sandy then told him that Gigi had been told recently that she was sick. He shrugged and said, "She looks fine to me."

Gay then had the following to say to all of them about auras and to Gigi, in particular, about the experience:

It is not from me you will learn the "meaning" of the colors, for they are quite individual and changeable as emotions. Trust the feelings and impressions [Steven's] for that is what is important here. The distance, of course, indicates the personal power and influence but this, of course, is again an interpretation. The colors are significant, but the meanings vary. Gigi, your health is, of course, an important consideration. Being in trance need not deplete energies, for never are you not in a trance. The trance states are simply altering consciousness and are not dissimilar to meditative states; however, your consideration needs to be toward what makes you feel good and strong. You need to give yourself permission to use the trance states solely for yourself and not feel pressure to perform. Give to yourself first. The suggestions on health are quite valid as stated; however, you must realize that even a psychic has underlying motives and prejudices — something it seems to be is a part of human existence. Stop putting others on pedestals and realize you have the power within you. Your health is not in such disastrous shape that you cannot do psychic work. The problem has to do with internal pressures. It is you who still feels inferior to others, and this woman simply tuned into this fear. You need to realize you do have strength. Concentrate slowly on strength rather than weakness. (9/6/80)

Again, the psychic had been accurate in picking up Gigi's concerns and fears. But because of her own particular interests and her own unique approach, she had presented the material in such a way that rather than giving Gigi positive material with which to work, she had created a negative reaction, immobilizing her for close to a month. She may have had fears about her own health and so, when she tied into Gigi's fears, her emphasis lay there. Gigi had been unable to take what was beneficial and reject what was not. Steven's innocent appraisal of her aura and Gay's emphasis on positive action pulled her out of her depression and, once again, she was able to center herself and begin to act assertively on her own behalf.

Sometimes people's misunderstanding about the kind of information that a psychic picks up causes undue fear. A young divorced woman with four children called Sheila one day, begging for an immediate appointment. She was so distressed that Sheila rearranged her schedule to see her as soon as possible. When the woman arrived, she explained that she was upset because of a recent visit to another psychic who had told her all about her children — except for one. The psychic had talked as if she only had three children, giving her a long and extensive rundown on each of them. Intimidated and upset, she had evidently left without clearing up the confusion. Several days had gone by and she became more and more worried that something was going to happen to the fourth child — perhaps even death — and that was why the psychic had not "seen" him. It was then that a friend recommended that she call Sheila. Gay explained:

> Good day. There is no need to worry about your children. There is one child whose energy is simply not as strong as the others. This child is much more withdrawn and remote. He has not been with you in other lives, whereas all three other children have been with you before. This child feels on the outside but does not express this feeling openly, and I feel more strongly the presence of other children around you. (6/19/80)

Gay then went on to explain the dynamics of her family patterns and gave her some suggestions for bringing harmony into her home. Sandy and Sheila explained to her that psychics work by "picking up" the energies around her, and so the other psychic had simply missed the weaker "frequency." Nothing was going to happen to her child. The distance, as Gay explained, was psychological and psychic. Knowing this, she could now take steps to correct the imbalance.

Another much more dramatic incident involved a young man who had periodically talked to Gay over the years. He was a sensitive man, curious and open, but occasionally ungrounded. He had gone to a psychic for a reading. At its close, the psychic told Donald that he was very sorry, but a negative entity had "slipped out" of him during the reading and attached itself to Donald. He further said that it would take Donald a lifetime to get rid of it. When he arrived at Sheila's, Donald was extremely upset because this "negative entity" had been having a detrimental effect on his life. He wanted to know how to protect himself and say no to its power over him. Gay spoke to him:

> Good day. Do not say no to "negative forces." Say yes to life and higher energies. To the extent that this energy has caused distress is the extent of your fear of your own power, your own strength and psychic abilities. This energy is no more harmful than energy from negative friends on the physical plane. It is not necessary to endure a lifetime of any pain or harm from this. You are free, and this moment is the time to realize this. Simply by asking to speak to me, you ask for higher energy and you are protecting your self. Trust. Send energy and love. Trust in your own power. (5/80)

Often people call who are upset because some psychic has told them of some dire event that is going to happen in their future. One woman called distressed because an astrologer had told her that a certain month was going to be crucial for her father, and that he may very well die. Another woman had had her cards read at a local restaurant, and the tarot reader had told her that someone close to her would die in the near future. The woman had just lost her father, and she was sure now that her mother would die as well. (The prediction was partially accurate, as is often the case, but the relative was a distant uncle who had been sick for a long time.) When these calls come to Sandy and Sheila, they explain their understanding of the future and the nature of predictions. Often Gay has said, as she did to a woman in November of 1979, the following concerning the future:

> There is no future as you think of the future. All is happening now. The present is all there is and contains everything that is thought to be the past and future. You are creating your future this instant and often future is influenced by what is past programming. That is why the future is not set. There are an infinite number of probabilities – each valid and real in their own reality.

When a psychic makes a prediction, therefore, he or she is picking up impressions of the strongest probabilities that may occur, based on the person's present beliefs, thoughts, emotions, and situation. That person has the power at any given moment to change course and thereby actualize different probabilities. The future is set by the present, and yet also totally free and undetermined, by virtue of one's personal power to create the reality of one's choosing. Because of the power of suggestion by a given authority (in this case, the psychic), the person hearing a prediction may feel it inevitable. Then, as a matter of course, actualizes that particular probability, thus proving the psychic right. That does not mean psychic predictions are wrong or inherently bad, but they should be understood as probabilities based on where the person is now in his or her life. If psychics would use the words, "I feel that there is a strong probability that you..." before each prediction, much distress and misunderstanding would be avoided. Gay has consistently refused to make predictions of any kind, telling people who ask questions about the future that they are the only creators of their destiny, and they alone determine what will or will not happen to them. When the prediction concerns someone other than the person addressed, as in the case of the woman who was told that her father may die during a certain month because of astrological influences, Gay explains the nature of influences and assures the person of everyone's right to create their own reality. In the case of the woman mentioned here, Gay told her that indeed her father was going to make some major decisions concerning his health, but they were his decisions to make, and it would be best if she simply meditated and sent him love, releasing him to be free to actualize his own future. Her worrying and "belief" in the certainty of the prediction would only send him negative energy and would make his own decision harder and less clear than it would be if she simply sent him love.

Sometimes people are frightened by their own visions. During the summer of 1980, a young woman from New York questioned her relationship with a long lost father. He had left her mother when she was a baby, and she had not had any physical contact with him during her life. Recently she had found herself thinking of him a lot and had experienced what she described as a "waking dream" in which she saw him lying dead in a coffin. The vision had been vivid and the accompanying emotions very strong, so she was convinced that he had died. She asked Gay for confirmation of this.

> Although distant on the physical plane, your father is close for he has been thinking of you recently. He has been ill. It seems to have something to do with the heart, and he fears death. This is what you saw. You saw his fear of death, and as psychic impressions occur, yours came in this way....You are very psychic yourself, and you need to continue to trust your impressions and thoughts. It is important not to take these impressions and visions literally, for often they are symbolic or represent deeper feelings. Trust them, yet also reflect quietly on their meaning.

Gay also gave her some personal information about how her need for her father had affected her relationships, and how this too was reflected in her vision.

Our beliefs, our thoughts, our emotions and feelings – all are reflected in the reality we create, whether that reality be on the physical plane, in dreams, or in our psychic experience. Reflecting quietly on the meaning of all experience, trusting that all experience is valid and real, is an important part of staying grounded as we open to the richness of an expanded consciousness. Without this reflection, this self-awareness, it is unfortunately much too easy to indulge in unwarranted fear or powerless flights doomed to crash. One close friend of Sandy's was experiencing much anger and confusion in her life as she went through a painful divorce. She was, at the same time, beginning to experience her own personal power and psychic ability. For a time, these two aspects of her life intermingled, with some unfortunate results. During one of her meditations, she had a vision in which a tornado hit the house where her three children still lived with their father. She became so convinced that this experience was definitely going to happen on such and such a day, that she talked her children into moving their valuables out of the house. Her estranged husband thought she had gone crazy and was very concerned for the children. The day passed and the tornado did not happen. She was perplexed. The vision was so clear, so vivid. What could have happened? The vision was real, Gay explained. She had indeed tapped in on a probability. However, in this case, it was a remote probability that she had drawn to her meditation, because of her anger at her husband and her guilt for leaving him. She had wanted it to happen so that, in some way, she would have been vindicated for what she then believed was her own "bad" behavior.

Another person who had felt powerless during most of her life began to see how indeed she did create her life and had the personal power to do so. She had come to Gay with the idea that she had been, in a previous incarnation, Marie Antoinette. Gay explained to her that she had had previous experience similar to this unfortunate queen. The woman chose not to hear this and chatted on about how a card reader had told her that she had actually been Marie Antoinette, confirming her own deepest beliefs. Gay talked to her about her beliefs about power — political power, in particular — and how, because she felt she had abused it in past lives, she now believed that all power must somehow be taken from her...by a beheading, if necessary. She heard what she had wanted to hear and left feeling very high and powerful. That was fine. However, she evidently did not choose to reflect on the meaning of this experience. A month or so later she called Sheila and asked her to contribute some writing to a venture she had begun that was going to save the world from its present course toward devastation. She also announced that she was now sure that she was Marie Antoinette, as she had just met the reincarnation of Louis XIV, and together they were going to right all wrongs. A month later she called, despondent because the entire venture had fallen through, and Louis XIV turned out to be a jerk.

During the summer of 1980, a friend of Sandy's loaned her a book called *Omens of Awareness* by David Tansley. Sandy glanced at it briefly and saw that it was about UFO encounters, but put it aside until she had time to read it. UFO's interested her but were not a major concern. Three days later, she and Sheila had a call from a woman who felt she was a UFO contactee. She wanted a session with Gay to "see if it was real." Sandy thought, "I guess I'm supposed to read that book." The woman came, however, before she had an opportunity to read very much. During her adult life, the woman had seen several flying objects in the skies around her home on the Jersey Shore. The experience that she was most concerned about, however, was more than a simple "sighting." She had gotten ready for bed one evening but, before retiring, was inexplicably drawn to the bedroom window. There again she saw a flying saucer. The UFO approached her apartment building and hovered there, extending a walkway to her balcony. Two men left the ship and walked into her bedroom, coming directly through the walls. She found that she was not frightened and even asked if she could also walk through walls. They answered, "Of course." She fell asleep sitting up, only to awaken hours later in her bed. The experience had been very real, but she had some doubts about its validity. She wanted to dismiss it as a dream, yet she was obsessed with the conviction that it was much more than that. She also wanted to know if she had been hypnotized or controlled in any way. What Gay had to say to her about this experience was lengthy. It is quoted here because of its relevance to many other kinds of psychic, as well as UFO, experience:

> You have been attempting to force your experience to meet a rational, intellectual standard of reality, just as you were forced to do as a child. You do indeed have a very vivid imagination, but that does not make experiences less real. As a child you were forced to keep your imaginative experiences to yourself. That was a result of the fears of those you were with. You were told not to trust your mind, and it was called "just imagination." Consequently, there is a need to prove to others how real your experiences are. There are many layers of reality and, at times, it is not possible to interpret one layer in terms of another. Your quest is to make others see that you are valid. The experience is your own, and it was indeed valid. You may not be able to prove this in an objective, scientific sense. The reality of your experience, however, is like a dream. Not that your experience was a dream, but it can be likened to a dream, for upon analysis it changes; and in retrospect, your perceptions and ideas about reality are placed upon this experience. Therefore, you have chosen to believe it is what your preconceived notions were already. Looking at what happened to you, first, you must trust your feelings and believe in yourself. There are many energies in the universe. The individuals you encountered were channeling energies from another source, and this was indeed a source in space. I feel that these individuals

in no way intended to harm. There are many energies that are reaching out to this planet and can be of help to many. You are simply very sensitive, and you also enjoy the drama of what happened to you. There may be fear, but I also sense that you wanted to be special. You have wanted something out of the ordinary. Many times you have been afflicted with boredom and periods of depression. I feel that you psychically drew this event to you to give you a feeling of participating in something special. It was indeed special, but you must let go of this and accept it for what it was – an exchange of energies. It was meant to bring to you new energy, to open you up. At the same time you welcomed this event, there was fear of this and a lack of trust in your own ability to handle this situation. I feel you were not harmed or even hypnotized. At least not formally. You often, however, hypnotize yourself at times of shock or stress. Hypnosis is not a mysterious force, as believed, to overpower others. It is simply an altering of consciousness. You did what you could do at the time, and I feel you have continued to receive these energies in dreams. The energy I am referring to is simply another kind of energy that many are used to. I do not feel any conscious attempt to control, more to give, but giving is often received with suspicion. In your individual case, it is quite difficult for you to receive and to even give to yourself.

The UFO contact was real. The angel in Sandy's bedroom was real. All of our experience is valid. What is important to realize is that all experience is valid in terms of our own beliefs, feelings and thoughts. Some of it corresponds to the physical reality and is scientifically provable. Some of it is not, but comes from other layers of reality which are often far richer in psychological and psychic implication than the "scientifically" approved world. After the woman left, Sandy read Tansley's book. His contention is that many UFO contacts – valid contacts – are the product of psychic energies drawn to those who, for their own complex and beautiful reasons, delve into realities not conventionally accepted on our physical plane.

Another common kind of ungrounded experience that often results from agitated states of emotional turmoil are "psychic storms." Sandy's first encounter with that idea was in the fall of 1977, when she was going through many difficult changes in her relationships with men in general, and with one in particular. Everything seemed to go crazy! She lost her address book. She lost one hundred dollars of Mind Matters money. The windshield wipers on her car kept going on and off for no reason. She kept hurting herself – not seriously, but bumps, bruises and little cuts. Nothing on her job worked out well – papers lost, appointments broken, people unavailable. She wondered what in the world was going on! Then she heard that the man she was "storming" with was experiencing similar events in his life. He had broken his glasses. His car was not working. His job was going badly. He continually complained that the whole world was coming apart! Sandy asked Gay what was going on.

> That man is influencing you more than you want to see. Angry thoughts create an atmosphere like a storm when they meet each other. Be calm, peaceful. These are two people creating angry thoughts which meet and cause this unrest and create the troublesome situations. (11/8/77)

This situation frequently occurs when unresolved feelings literally fly through psychic skies. Both Sandy and her friend were refusing to deal directly with their feelings. This created a psychic storm, making it difficult to remain balanced and centered in their daily lives, even though they had no physical contact during that time.

"What! You contacted Gay on a Ouija Board? I've been warned about Ouija Boards. They're dangerous!" Many times over the years, Sheila and Sandy would hear this response when they would describe their initial encounter with Gay Bonner. At first they could not understand the vehemence of the board's detractors. They had had no untoward experiences with the Ouija and neither had Jane Roberts, who had first contacted Seth with one. Later they were to read accounts of people who had been "tricked," "seduced" or in some way traumatized by "evil" spirits who, it seemed, jumped at the chance to control these poor unwitting beings who opened themselves to such chicanery by using the Ouija. The Ouija Board is a medium; however, rather than being its own message, it is simply an open channel between energies. The operators of a Ouija will draw energies to themselves, according to their own beliefs, thoughts, and feelings. If the board is approached with fear, then an appropriate form of energy will cooperatively communicate by scaring the expectant participants. Anger will attract anger. Joy will attract joy. Any method, whether it be a Ouija Board, automatic writing, deep meditation, trance mediumship, or whatever, is only a medium or channel. The participants always determine the quality of the material coming through the channel, as it reflects their deepest personal beliefs.

In 1977, Sheila had worked with two young women who were experimenting with a Ouija Board. They had contacted an entity who called himself a guide and who daily told them what to do in their lives — who they should go out with, what they should do in terms of their work, how they should raise their children, and so on. The information was specific and often contained predictions as to what was going to happen in a coming week. Often the advice and the predictions worked — especially in the beginning. Then, as the women became more and more dependent upon the advice, things started to go wrong. Predictions were wrong. Decisions as to how to live began to become bizarre. The women were taking it all very seriously and had stopped living their own lives. They were "controlled" by some unknown entity who called himself Sam. When they finally came to Sheila with their distress, she asked them if they allowed others in their physical lives to tell them how to live? "You are the only ones, living or dead, who know what is best for you. Why do you give away your power to anyone?" It took them several months, but they finally caught on and, with a great deal of anger, threw away the board, convinced that it was the "bad guy" and that they had been duped.

In July of 1979, Gay spoke to a couple who had come with a question about their use of a Ouija Board. Their board had told them that their dog, who was quite old, would die on October 4th of that year. They wanted to know how reliable that information was.

> Continue to use the board, but do not take the messages in too literal a translation for they are constantly being filtered through your own consciousness and belief system, which will become clearer with practice. You will continue to learn about your deepest beliefs, for you will see them reflected in the messages you receive. You need to practice and listen carefully. Simply do the work, then leave the messages alone. You try to analyze too much. Simply enjoy and have fun. Always at the start, your own consciousness is there and, with practice, the belief system operating in the physical focus you have chosen can be set aside and the messages will be clearer. By clearer, I do not mean more specific, but clearer in terms of the feelings and guidance they provide. For example, the date given you about your dog was included because you need the specifics now. At least having specific knowledge makes you feel more secure. That date is not a set thing at all. It is, however, set in a probable reality. There is this happening occurring in a reality that is not necessarily the one that you and your dog are currently focused in. In one sense your message is valid, as all of these psychic messages are; but on the other hand, there need be no cause for alarm. Your dog is in a transitional period of her life. I see physical powers fading, but she is not yet ready to die.

Some days very tired, and she does slip in and out of the physical world, but I do not see this as occurring this soon. The message came on a day that your dog's consciousness was out of her body most of the day. She practices, as people do, these other realities that may be encountered after death. You picked this day to receive this message, and the specifics are things you want and need now, so they are given.

Clarity is important. So is discrimination. Whenever a person chooses to seek advice or information from any source, that person is ultimately responsible for deciding what is applicable or appropriate for his or her self. A young woman, asking about certain questionable guides that her boyfriend had been contacting through a Ouija Board and automatic writing, heard the following from Gay:

> There are no good or bad guides. Simply guides. Guides are not different than physical friends. The guides you have are ones you draw to you psychically, and they will reflect your inner state. I see that these guides are simply entities who have had similar problems in other lifetimes and are stuck still in the emotions generated from the thought patterns and experiences. They have gravitated to your friend because of similar situations. Any entity can be a guide. It is simply a question of discriminating the content of the communication. As you discriminate on a physical plane, so it is on the spiritual and mental levels. (11/1/79)

Many influences surround us as we move through our lives. These influences can affect us negatively or positively, depending on our own states of mind. The more aware we are of our own selves, the more easily we can choose the quality of the influences around us. Becoming aware of influences — the thoughts and feelings of others; our own aspects, such as past lives, other selves, even future selves; astrological factors; personal beliefs about health; beliefs and concepts gleaned from religious leaders, parents, or any authoritative figure; any of the myriad of sensory data entering our consciousness on any given day — is an important part of taking active responsibility for creating a positive reality. As we learn to be aware, it is sometimes important to give ourselves some help. Sheila and Sandy learned very early that they needed help in the form of spiritual protection — symbolic thought forms created specifically to screen out negative input, whether the input originates from one's own thoughts and beliefs or comes from the "outside": the oral suggestions of others, the moods and thoughts of those around us, the anger or jealousy that others may direct toward us. Much of the process of opening psychically involves becoming aware of others' thoughts and feelings. It is important, therefore, to be especially aware of the possible effects of this.

Gay began urging the women to use a technique in their daily meditative practices, in order to protect themselves from unwanted psychic influences. The process is simple. Imagine white light surrounding your body and mind. Know that this white light is a symbol of spiritual protection and, as such, will screen out negative influences while allowing all positive thought and feeling to enter. Many people build psychic and psychological walls around themselves to protect their sensitive natures. Unfortunately, walls block out everything – keeping out love as well as harmful effects. Consciously using white light as a selective screen that bounces away negativity and absorbs positive influence makes such walls unnecessary. Gay has suggested to several people who have unconsciously "built" walls around themselves that they consciously tear down these walls, block by block, daily replacing them with white light. As the conscious, positive thought form replaces the old, limiting one, positive changes could occur in their lives. Although Sandy and Sheila did not have to tear down walls, they found that using the light daily had a tremendous impact on their lives.

All her life, Sheila had unwittingly taken on the thoughts and moods of those around her. She would often go into a roomful of people and suddenly find her mood changed; unfortunately, the change was often from high to low. She never understood this and usually blamed herself for being too sensitive or moody. She would often find herself angry when someone around her was angry, or depressed when another was depressed. It was not until she began her psychic work that she realized what had been happening. Her sensitivity became even more apparent after she began the readings, for not only would she pick up on people's feelings, she would also pick up their physical symptoms. As she began working consciously with the white light as psychic protection, she found that she was able to immediately discern when the mood or symptom was hers or another's. This intuitive ability was very real, and she began to trust her thoughts and feelings as she asked for feedback from those around her. She found that indeed she was correctly discriminating between what were her own feelings and symptoms and what belonged to others.

At first, Sandy thought this was fine for Sheila but did not think it was necessary for herself. She felt she was less sensitive and, therefore, less apt to pick up on others. Gay continued to urge her to use the light, however, and eventually she did. She too found that it made a tremendous difference in her emotional relations with others. She too began to quickly discern others' "trips." She then stopped taking them on as her own. Sandy realized that this was something she had been doing all of her life. The protection worked in many areas of their lives, but the biggest change was in this ability to discriminate between their own thoughts and feelings and the input of others around them.

Sheila found out how "real" the white light had become in her life. It was not only a subtle influence in her relationships with others, but it was a visible part of her. As she usually does not visualize during her hypnosis or meditation sessions, she would simply "think" the light around her and trust that it was indeed there. During the summer of 1979, she was working parttime in a restaurant in New Hope, Pennsylvania, where she was living. Her work as a psychic was generally known to her fellow workers and the regular customers in the restaurant. One very young woman working there during her summer break from college had made an appointment for a reading. She was very excited about it, but also very apprehensive, as she had had no previous experience with psychics. One day she was talking to one of the customers she waited on and mentioned her upcoming appointment with Sheila and Sandy. The man, it turned out, was an amateur psychic himself who said he read auras. He looked over at Sheila and turned to the girl saying, "I don't know if you should go to her. She may be quite unclear because her aura has two colors in it – white and gold. Auras should be only one color." The girl became quite concerned. She finally approached Sheila with her apprehensions. Sheila began to laugh. She explained that the man evidently had some definite, but perhaps confused, beliefs about the nature of auras and that the reason he had seen two colors was because she daily used them in her meditations. She would first "think" gold light entering her body from the universe, then "think" white light coming out of her body and surrounding it an aura of spiritual protection. The girl came and had a very successful session with Gay. Sheila was delighted, in spite of the man's misinterpretation, to find that her thought forms were indeed real and visible.

Sheila and Sandy usually apply their white light protection during their daily meditations as part of their procedure. How it is done, however, does not matter. Occasionally Gay will tell someone to "think" it on while they put their clothes on every morning. For others, an elaborate, conscious ritual may be appropriate. What is important is to recognize the value of conscious spiritual protection that is open to positive influence but deflects negativity. Sometimes the suggestions from Gay are very specific on the subject. One woman who came for a session had been doing therapy with physically handicapped and emotionally disturbed children. She was very effective in her work, but often extremely tired and run down. Gay gave her the following advice:

> It is very important for you to know that because you have this healing energy, you often absorb others' pain — that of the children you work with—and also emotional pain. You need to be aware of this and to consciously let go of the pain each day. See, when you touch others, the positive energy flowing into your head and out your hands. The pain does enter your body, but see it also leaving your body through your feet. See it as a grey light which leaves your body. Picture it leaving your feet and then being absorbed into the earth's energy, which can reactivate this pain into a positive form. Your body does not need this, and I feel it is psychically induced. This procedure will ease much of the physical pain also. Then see your body surrounded by a white light. This light is a shield against negative energies entering your body and even the emotional pain you are absorbing. (4/22/79)

As time went on, Sheila and Sandy learned that thought forms such as white light began to do more than simply protect against discomfort, either psychically or physically. They found that they began to draw people to them who were normally positive and loving — people who gave them positive energy and feedback. The white light, then, became a positive draw rather than a negative screen. When negative influences did enter their lives, however, they found that they were immediately able to see the lesson that was there for them. They became more conscious of their reality.

Just as white-light spiritual protection helped the women to clarify their interactions with other people by separating their thoughts and feelings from those of others, they found at times that other techniques were occasionally needed to handle the influx of new data coming from their psychic adventures. At one point during 1978, Gay admonished them for valuing their daily trance time over their physical reality.

> You both must remember your physical experiences are as valid as trance states. Some people think only physical experience valid. You two have the opposite problem. In your creative aspects, everything is valid. From here your reality is a trance state. (5/20/78)

They realized that she was right. They had become so ena-
mored with the psychic experiences they had been having during
trance states, that they had been paying little attention to the physical
events of their everyday lives — especially, its input into their creative
endeavors. They were, at that point, ungrounded. This happens occasionally to those coming to them for sessions with Gay or Sheila's ESP
classes. Most of the people are just beginning to expand their awareness and find that they can explore wider subjective realities than they
had ever thought possible. They wanted to be less grounded, less
"logical," less "realistic," less "intellectual." For most, the struggle is
more to let go of these ways of being in the world. For some, however,
the opposite is the problem. They take off and fly into inner spaces that
can threaten their ability to function on earth. For those people, simple
grounding exercises are often necessary. One Sheila uses in her classes
is a simple visualization where the class participants see themselves
rooted to the earth as if they were huge, sturdy trees. Their branches
reach out and explore new realities, while their roots keep them firmly
tied to earth. Sandy found a simple grounding technique in Ram Dass'
Being There. She would stop herself wherever she might be during her
day (usually off in a daydream or fantasy) and ask "Where am I?" The
answer is always, "Here." Then, "What time is it?" Always answering
"Now." This simple inner dialogue would immediately pull her to full
awareness of her physical reality on earth.

Another technique that Sandy found very helpful, when incom-
ing psychic data and experience was too overwhelming to digest or too
incomprehensible to accept at the moment, was a device she created
drawing from Samuel Coleridge's idea that when we read literature,
we "willingly suspend our disbelief." She would take any new experience or information that she could not readily assimilate and, rather
than dismiss it or automatically disbelieve it because it was strange,
would place it in a huge bag she visualized hanging just to the right,
over her head. This bag was her conscious, "willing suspension of
disbelief." She was not ready to believe what was there, but she was
also not going to throw it all away as nonsense or unbelievable. As her
understanding and experience eventually brought this data into a perspective she could assimilate, she would drop it into her area of belief,
positioned somewhere in her head and heart area. This device has
served her well during the tremendous changes in her beliefs and
consciousness over the past few years. She could remain open to new
experience and new concepts without rushing into a premature, and
perhaps naive, acceptance of everything coming her way. She also

found that the confusion some people experience due to the rapid influx of new ideas that conflict with their old, established cultural beliefs, was lessened for her because of her conscious, suspended bag of disbeliefs.

Staying grounded as you expand psychically requires self awareness, discrimination, and most of all, trust in yourself. You are the only final authority as to what is real for you and how that reality is best understood for your own growth.

Chapter 12

Seeking Quiet States:
HOW AND WHY

ON JULY 21, 1979, Sandy and Sheila settled down in Sandy's living room to have a private session with Gay. Sheila said that she had been having persistent thoughts during the week about the meaning of Gay's name. "I know she told us that Gay Bonner was the name she had when we knew her in 18th Century Wales," Sheila remarked, "but lately I've had a feeling that it means much more than that to her. The words 'God As You' keep popping into my mind. I feel she has something to say about it." She did.

> You did know me by this name, Gay, when we first met; but I chose my name even then. My intent is to perceive God As You and to address individuals in this manner, ultimately to raise their belief in what God is — The 'X' I referred to [earlier in our communications] — You stand in this center of X always and radiate in all directions as God As You, and so I hope to see this as I speak to the many you have provided for me. You see, there are many dimensions and possibilities, even in a name seemingly picked from nowhere but extremely significant. Everything has significance. No accidents.

Even in a name, we may discover new dimensions and possibilities. In each individual, therefore, lay the potential for this discovery that requires only our attention. Every willing person has the ability to explore the many-faceted jewel of his or her complex and dynamic consciousness, to discover wider, deeper and richer portions of a larger and ever-expanding Self that is indeed God As You. Most of us — in our outward-looking, hectic Western culture — must learn to find quiet, so that we can pay attention.

As described in the beginning of this book, Sheila and Sandy found their quiet through different methods. Sheila began with a self-hypnosis technique she learned in a book. Sandy started with a mantra and a few instructions from her therapist. After they had begun working together, they found that either method could lead them to the same result — similar, though certainly subjective, altered states of consciousness. In those altered states they found their usual busy, reasoning, logical selves moved aside, allowing other, untapped portions of their consciousness to communicate. Sandy would find herself flowing through images and feelings that were far removed from her usual consciousness, offering her a rich source of creative insight and symbols. Sheila's initial efforts were directed toward achieving profound physical relaxation in order to have a clear, relaxed, and uncluttered mind.

When they began to use hypnosis tapes and programming techniques, Sheila easily adapted to this procedure. Sandy had difficulty with the idea of programming, as she thoroughly enjoyed her free-floating meditations. They realized that both methods could lead to deep physical relaxation and a quiet mind, but that one was accomplished through a prescribed and purposeful procedure, and the other through intense concentration on a single word or idea. Sandy recognized the value of self-hypnosis programming so she developed a compromise. She would use the hypnosis procedure to take herself into a trance (altered state of consciousness), to program affirmations and visualizations, and would then let herself go and float freely, as she had always done in her meditations. That compromise worked well, and allowed her the flexibility of methods that she would later share with participants at Mind Matters seminars. As time went by, both women learned to shorten the procedures for going into trance. Eventually it became a question of knowing states of consciousness and going there, just as one knows physical places upon the earth and goes to them.

No one method or procedure is better than any other. Indeed, although each individual should seek whatever way is best for him or her, there are a few suggestions that may help the reader begin to learn to be quiet in order to pay attention to make his or her own discoveries.

First of all, it is most important to give yourself the time to be quiet. The amount of time is not important, but taking it is. This time should be uncluttered — both mentally and physically. Ask those around you to respect your need for your allotted time. For several years, Sandy had a handwritten sign tacked to her bedroom door which read, "Meditating Mother. Do not disturb." Her children soon learned that if she was allowed this time, she was much easier to live with, calmer, and more open to their interests. Mentally, it is important to set aside daily concerns: nagging grocery lists, dying grandmothers, job assignments, crumbling marriages, whatever. This may sound impossible, and perhaps even selfish, but the advantages to be gained in doing so will soon be evident in the increasingly efficient and caring manner with which you begin to handle these concerns. There are many tricks to aid you in giving yourself free time from mental involvements. You can simply suspend them, asking them to wait until you are finished. If a visualization helps, see yourself place your concerns on a high shelf until you are ready to resume their care. A locked box is another recommended method. Do not try to banish them from your life completely. Recognize that your daily concerns are there for a purpose and are a part of you. You will let them go as you finish with them.

The next consideration is physical comfort. You may wish to lie down. If so, see that your clothing is loose and comfortable, and be sure not to cross your legs. As you move into deeper states of consciousness, you will find that your body will grow heavier and crossed legs will be uncomfortable. Sitting up in a straightbacked chair may be a better alternative, as you may find yourself going into a natural sleep, especially if you are tired to begin with. Sandy and Sheila both found that as they became proficient at going into deeper and deeper trances, it became necessary not only to sit up but to sit cross-legged in a traditional yoga position. They found that they otherwise tended to "go too far" and, consequently, were unable to retain memory of their explorations. This is, however, an individual choice. The only requirement is comfort.

Once comfortable, your next decision is how to get "there." Always begin with a few deep breaths. This brings fresh oxygen into your physical body, so that it can effectively relax while your mind remains alert. You may then wish to concentrate on a word or phrase, keeping only that in mind. If you find your thoughts wandering elsewhere — to the grocery list, for instance — simply return your concentration to the word or phrase. Another method, similar in effect, is to concentrate on your breathing, watching your breath move in and out of your body. It is easier if you concentrate on a particular part of your breathing apparatus — your nostrils or your abdomen. A method Sandy has found useful when there has been a lot of outside distraction, is to simply concentrate on everything. Every noise, every creak,

every horn blowing, kid screaming, refrigerator slamming, cat meow-
ing, and dog barking can be a point of concentration. The effect is the
same. Soon you find yourself "there."

If you find you like a visual procedure for going into trance, any
of the self-hypnosis procedures may suit you. Progressive bodily relaxation is especially helpful if your body is usually tense. Begin with your
toes and feel or visualize a relaxation move into your feet, through
your ankles, your calves, your thighs, your hips, then into your fingers,
hands, forearms, upper arms, shoulders. Then move your attention to
the base of your spine and feel the relaxation move up, gradually
relaxing each part of the trunk of your body, flowing into your neck,
your scalp, and then draining down into your facial muscles. Be aware
of your eyes as muscles, and let them drop into your head. Relax your
jaw, leaving a space between your teeth. After you have completed this
process, run your consciousness back through your body, feeling the
complete relaxation as it has overtaken your physical form. This process may take practice, but eventually you will be able to think the
words "body relax," and the effect will simply wash over you.

After your physical body is completely relaxed, concentrate on
moving your consciousness to a deeper state. Again, there are many
methods for doing this. One of the most effective is to see yourself in a
situation in which you are going down. You may wish to imagine
yourself walking down a meadowy slope, a circular staircase, or a
rocky mountainside somewhere, which requires your utmost attention. You may wish to feel yourself falling through space, diving down
through water, or whatever your imagination provides. As you do,
count backwards, concentrating on the numbers. Sandy usually begins
with seven; counting "seven, down, down, down, deeper, deeper,
deeper; six, down, down, down, deeper, deeper, deeper," and so on,
until the count of one. The rhythmic repetition and concentration on
the up-coming number will usually take you rapidly into an altered
state. Once there, you may concentrate on visualizations or affirmations that you have developed to create a more satisfying reality;
or you may simply wish to float freely, feeling the peace of such profound relaxation and experiencing the flow of spontaneous communication which your subconscious may send your way. It is in these quiet
moments that you begin to discover who you really are — your many
dimensions and possibilities.

Once you have reached your unique, altered state of consciousness, expect anything, everything, and nothing. Your body will be
relaxed, your mind quiet. The clitter-clatter of your conscious mind

(or ego, if you prefer) will be quiet. You may see your thoughts float by. You are aware but unconcerned and detached. You may find dramas, in which you may or may not be involved, occurring in front of your inner vision. You may feel wonderful feelings of love and a sense of profound peace – an "all's right with the world" feeling. You may enter your body and experience your physical self from the inside, traveling with your blood or your breath. A half hour may feel like five minutes.

When you first begin practicing some form of deep relaxation, you may find that you are easily distracted, and irritated by disturbances. As you practice, however, you will see that this changes, and soon the disturbances will pass through you without affecting you. You will note the cat's meow or the child's shout, but you will be unconcerned and your concentration will not be interrupted. (If something is happening of immediate concern to you, however, you will respond appropriately, of course. You will not sit quietly as the house burns down! Your conscious or ego mind will immediately reassert its autonomy.)

If you are being guided by a hypnotist or teacher, you may find that you can easily communicate what you are experiencing. You may explore many different realities; and if someone questions you as you move through these realities, this will help you to stay focused and retain the memory of your experiences. A hypnotist is not necessary, however. You can make the explorations by yourself.

You may find that nothing happens. You may sit or lie down for your prescribed amount of time and feel nothing is happening. That too is okay. The quiet time will eventually have an effect on your life. You may simply find that your life is smoother. Answers may come faster than before. Your emotional reactions to events and people may be calmer and more appropriate. Stay with it, and these intangible benefits will become evident.

There is no one "right" method for journeying inward. The suggestions given above have worked for Sandy and Sheila and others they have known. Everyone must find his or her own way. Gay has stressed many different methods for different people. Sometimes the methods are physical. She may tell someone to run to relax. Sandy has a friend who runs seven or eight miles every morning and claims that his running is the best meditation he has every tried. Dance is another physical activity that Gay has frequently suggested as a form of meditation. Any sport requiring total concentration and involvement can bring the needed mental relaxation to clear the mind. Sometimes Gay suggests listening to music — especially classical music. Usually the person listening to Gay will respond with enthusiasm, "Yes, I've always loved Bach, but I've never thought of using music as a point of concentration."

One of the most appreciated parts of a session with Gay are the personal suggestions she often gives for meditation. Usually these suggestions are immediately recognized in some way by the recipient as a preference (as with Bach), a memory, or sometimes even a psychological aid. Sandy's meditation from Gay was such an aid:

> Your meditation technique is a flowing river. Sit on the bank and see water flowing by you. It knows not the direction but travels it anyway, which is what you are doing.

Sandy often forgets that simple truth and becomes caught in too much futuristic planning, worrying about what will happen and how. The flowing river reminds her that her life can flow spontaneously and yet as purposefully as it does.

Sheila's meditation was a setting among pine trees. These tall, slender, graceful trees offer her a sense of peace and a feeling of being grounded firmly on the earth. At the time Gay suggested this for meditation, Sheila lived in an apartment in a private house surrounded by pine trees. She realized how much comfort these trees gave her.

A friend of Sandy's, who was visiting from Nova Scotia, was talking to Gay in January of 1978. He asked if he could meditate.

> Yes, if you will learn to turn off the brooding type of thoughts. They will stop if you picture the sea; it is very calm and tranquil. You can even enter the sea and see yourself going down under the sea. It is peaceful and tranquil there, and beautiful; you will feel the presence of something quite spiritual. It is warm and comforting to you.

When Sheila came out of the trance, John was staring at her, amazed. "When you described going under the sea" he explained, "you were describing an experience I had the first time I ever went scuba diving, just this last summer. I loved it; and when I dove under the water, I felt such a profound feeling of peace!"

Sometimes the memories evoked by Gay's suggestions were much older. One woman was told to meditate in an apple orchard

> ...with blossoms in spring. Sit under the trees. Feel warm spring and smell. Do this in your mind. It will bring back peaceful memories. (3/18/78)

It did. The woman recalled a favorite place where, as a child, she would go to be alone and play out her fantasies. Many of Gay's suggestions for meditation are found in nature, color, or even our own bodies. A few are quoted here:

> You can simply relax using the sounds of rain falling, and in a gentle fashion. The day is grey, yet peaceful. Use this image in your mind, and it will relax you. It is enough to just feel calmness. If you do this every day, it needn't be a long exercise. Use the word 'peace' and then see the peaceful effect of rain. It can indeed be peaceful, and know a rainbow is beyond. (3/29/78)

> Use the setting of the sea. Concentrate on the seashore: sounds, smells, sights. Go there mentally to relax. It is a peaceful place for you. I see a house there, set off by itself, surrounded by sand dunes and stillness and quiet. (11/5/78)

> Trust your thoughts and use the flowers as points of concentration. The concentrating will enable you to relax. (3/5/80)

> In your relaxation, you need to imagine a peaceful place. This place is near water — a stream running through a meadow — with a waterfall. See this in your mind and allow the water to purify your soul. It will act also on healing your body. See this, and concentrate on the flowing water. Let it bring healing powers to you. (12/6/79)

> Use the method of concentrating on a piece of crystal. Simply concentrate on the beauty and simplicity of this and the many colors that can be reflected as sunlight hits the crystal. (6/24/78)

> I feel that meditating on the trees in a forest would be very helpful to you. Trees give you much energy. Use them both in a physical sense and in your mind to meditate on. The birch tree is a very good tree for you. It can give you much energy, but all trees respond to you and can give you much. (6/19/79)

> Meditate on the water. I see that water is very soothing for you. The seashore or perhaps near a stream. I also feel that the color green is a very good color for you. Use this color even more than you do, for it has quite soothing qualities. The Spring is your time of the year, for it brings new life. In your mind, use the color and create peaceful scenes around what I described. I also see a pink flowering bush that can give you a lightness of spirit. (11/29/79)

> To contact your higher self for guidance, simply concentrate and meditate using the color violet. This is a good color for you. The flower is also a good symbol for you. Quiet the mind. Think about this color, surrounding yourself with its vibrations, then trust your thoughts. (6/5/80)

You are indeed alone, as every soul is its own extension of a greater soul that covers the entire field of energy; thus you are a part of every living creature and everything that exists. You are the air and the sea and the sky, and the plants and animals you have eaten. Feel the air as it moves in you. It is, then, part of you; but as easily moves out to become a part of someone or something else. You are this also, and thoughts are the same. They move in and out of you. Then out and over to another—only what makes it different is the screen or mask that filters these thoughts; but thoughts are a part of all, and you are alone in that you are unique; but you are very closely linked to everything that exists. You are no different than the chair you sit on. There is no outside or inside. I say all this because you need to read and think on this; then you will find God in you – the unknown source of energy – and this energy will find you and set you free. Use the description of air and matter around you and concentrate on this, too. Begin to relax. Think only of the air you breathe in and out. See it as your thoughts coming in and out also. (3/29/78)

Being where you are is the ultimate meditation. Gay gave Sandy another method on the day she suggested the river. Sandy finds this meditation much more difficult but realizes that all of the inner work that she and Sheila have been doing is leading to such a state of consciousness.

Try an experiment. Take each day. Try one day at first and force yourself, as though you were meditating, to fully concentrate on every part of the day. Be where you are, and do not let any thoughts as to how you are doing enter. See what happens that day. (3/25/78)

As awareness of the many dimensions and possibilities of consciousness expands, each individual experiences his or her own unique inner world. No one can tell another whether or not his or her experience is "right" or "valid," as all inner experience is valid for each person. Although each of us must chart our own way through inner explorations, others' experiences can offer guideposts. Dick Sutphen discusses three different mind levels.[1] These levels are arbitrary, and certainly intermingle; but they are convenient as possible guidelines. The conscious mind contains will, reason, logic, and the five physical senses. Here is where we usually focus our attention. The subconscious mind stores all our memories from this life or past lives, our

---

[1] *You Were Born Again to Be Together*, p. 244.

habit patterns, our emotions – the "programming" that creates our responses to life on the physical level. It is this area that we usually first meet when we begin to explore the varied parts of our consciousness. Memories of a long-forgotten childhood event may surface. Flashes from dramas that could be associated with what we may call past-life aspects of ourselves may occur. Patterns in our lives may become obvious. The third level is what Dick calls the super-conscious mind, or higher self, which contains our creativity, our higher imaginative abilities, our psychic abilities, our feelings of a spiritual nature, our most intimate self-wisdom. This state of consciousness is often reached spontaneously during deep states of meditation or self hypnosis. You may feel yourself pulled up and out of your usual physical dimensions into an expanded state of awareness, where you experience intense feelings of love and peace. Often this state of consciousness is experienced with a sense of white or gold light. It is this state which is most conducive to what Sandy and Sheila have described as guide contact in Chapter 5 of this book.

If higher-self states are not reached spontaneously, the practiced meditator can learn to move him or herself to these levels of consciousness. Once you have reached a state of deep, physical relaxation with a quiet mind, as described above, you can consciously move yourself into expanded, higher-self states by letting go of the physical, manifest world and floating upward. Sandy and Sheila most frequently use a counting technique. Count from one to eight or ten, visualizing yourself letting go and floating up and out. With each count you will let go more and more of your physical awareness and move toward a white or gold light. On the final count step out into the light. With practice, you will eventually be "there." First, simply enjoy the peace and contentment in which you find yourself. Here you can ask for your guides to make themselves known to you. If there is any question that you may have about yourself or your life, ask that question and then be quiet. The answer may come in words, images, symbols, or feelings. Occasionally Sandy finds that the answers are delayed, coming sometime after she has come out of trance. The most important thing to remember is to trust your mind. Trust whatever comes to you and do not judge. Just let it be, and eventually you will understand.

Sandy had been working weekly with a young woman who was seeking to expand her conscious awareness of her creative processes. A healer, specializing in Shiatsu therapy, she desired to learn more about various forms of healing. She felt that she could tap her own creative aspects for direction and specific knowledge of techniques that she may have known in previous lifetimes. The weekly sessions were successful, and she eventually learned to channel information from her own higher self. Early in the sessions, during a time when she was having doubts about the validity of her channeled information, Gay said the following to her:

> In this reality there is no distinction between what is valid and what is imagination. It is in the culture and reality that you normally reside in that these distinctions appear to be important. Imagination is not to be trusted. Thoughts are discarded because they are just imagination, and yet your entire reality is built upon your imagination, which is indeed a beautiful thing. Imagination is not something that needs to be put on a shelf and discounted. Rather it needs to be celebrated. It matters not what you specifically say from the higher self, for the ultimate judge of its worth is in how you feel and how it begins to effect your physical reality. It is important, as I said, not to tear apart the material and attempt to sort out what is valid. From this reality, I see nothing invalid, and you need to take this perspective upon examining what you have done. It makes no sense to examine your transmissions with the idea of sorting out what is right, what is wrong, for it does not matter. You have, of course, expressed many of your feelings in these sessions, but this is also quite valid. Simply continue to practice. You inhibit yourself by analyzing too much. You want to continue to look outside, and yet you know that all the answers are within yourself. You are an aspect of God, and as such you have the responsibility to love this part of you. (8/19/80)

Trust your mind. Do not judge. Ultimately the true judgment of whatever you receive is in the effect upon your feelings and your physical reality. It is in this suspension of judgment that we can allow ourselves the freedom to expand and grow in awareness of our dimensions and possibilities. In doing this, we become aware of our spiritual being. In a long private session on October 4, 1980, Gay said the following to Sandy, Sheila, and a friend, Ginny, regarding their spiritual natures and the importance of following their own unique spiritual paths:

> Do not compare your spiritual being or nature with others. Let them also be how they are too. You need to realize that spiritualness is a condition not bound by restrictions or rules. Do what you want to do. Be of the physical world, and you will learn the nature of your being. Being alive is being creative. You need do nothing

but affirm your aliveness. If you affirm living, if you decide to participate wholly in being alive, you will not need to concern yourself with meditations per se. The lesson is in how not to judge your spiritual beings. Yes, many again think that there is a particular method or way that works. No one reaches full aliveness using another's method. Deep frustration and unhappiness is often the result, until one begins to surrender and say yes to life; yes to the self that is God. For in following someone else's plan, chaos results; but the learning is also as deep as the frustration, for the end is seeing it is you. The problem has been that there are those who reached this understanding; however, they were looked upon as knowing answers for all others. Their lives were studiously observed and copied. However, this is not the way. Drop all ways. See all ways as pointing to God, but realize you are God and you can be nothing else but God. Affirming life is the key here. You will each know what to do with your lives.

It is each individual's responsibility, then, to discover who he or she is, for we are all aspects of God. "God as You," from Gay's perspective. Knowing that, we know what to do with our lives. This learning has lead Sheila and Sandy to a new understanding of their relationship, not only to each other and to their friends, but to the entire planet. Expanding individual awareness expands global consciousness. As each person makes his own discovery of his creative potential, he adds to the total awareness of all on earth. As we all become aware that we are creating the earth as it is now, we will take conscious responsibility for its condition.

There is much talk of a New Age Consciousness – a planetary consciousness that is more ecologically, socially and spiritually balanced. If such a vision is to be attained, the beginning is with every one of us. David Spangler, speaking in an interview published in the *Yoga Journal*,[2] said the following:

> If I don't feel it is possible for me as a person to change and gain a new vision of my world and myself, then it will be more difficult for me to accept such a possibility for my culture....A quantum leap – a transformation – into a different future, one of inner control and outer harmonization and mutual support, seems to a person who goes along with linear projections as only so much utopian wishful thinking. Once I experience the possibility – and the actuality – of such transformation in my personal life, how-

---

[2] The New Age Phenomenon: A Conversation with David Spangler, *Yoga Journal*, January-February 1980, pp. 16-17.

ever, I have some basis for conceiving it and working for it in my society. That is why so many aspects of the New Age movement focus on inner change and the experience of personal transformation as the first step in building a new culture. The idea of a new Age says to many people that it is all possible, and therefore worthwhile to take such steps.

Discover you are more than you think you are. Discover your psychic nature, your creative nature, your "God As You" nature. Travel inward and discover the joy of your being. It is this personal journey which can move us all toward a world of love and cooperation.

Suggested Reading

The following list includes only those books mentioned throughout this book. This is only a starting place, for there are many excellent books available on expanding consciousness. By all means, read all of Jane Roberts' and David Spangler's books. Visit your bookstore and peruse the occult, religious, psychology, science/mind, and spiritual sections. As you read and explore, you will find the material will come to you from all directions, as if by some magical source unleashed by your seeking, pouring forth to gently fill you, always with the appropriate intensity, at the right time.

Bach, Richard, *Illusions: the Adventures of a Reluctant Messiah,* (Delacorte, 1977).

Bentov, Itzhak, *Stalking the Wild Pendulum,* (Dutton, 1977).

Besant, Annie, and C. W. Leadbeater, *Thought-Forms,* (quest, 1969).

Capra, Fritjof, *The Tao of Physics,* (Shambhala, 1975).

Hawken, Paul, *The Magic of Findhorn,* (Harper & Row, 1975).

Leonard, George B, *The Transformation,* (Dell, 1972).

LeShan, Lawence, *The Medium, the Mystic, and the Physicist,* (Ballantine, 1975).

Lilly, John C., MD, *The Center of the Cyclone,* (Julian Press, 1972).

Monroe, Robert A., *Journeys Out of the Body,* (Doubleday, 1971).

Ram Dass, *Being There* (Crown Press, 1971).

Roberts, Jane, *The Seth Material,* (Prentice Hall, 1970);
  The Nature of Personal Reality, (Prentice Hall, 1974);
  Adventures in Consciousness, (Prentice Hall, 1975);
  Psychic Politics, (Prentice Hall, 1976);
  The World View of Paul Cezanne, (Prentice Hall, 1977);
  The Afterdeath Journal of an American Philosopher: The World View of William James, (Prentice Hall, 1978);
  The "Unknown" Reality, Vol. I & II, (Prentice Hall, 1977,79).

Smith, Adam, *Powers of Mind,* (Random House, 1975).

Spangler, David, *The Laws of Manifestation,* (Findhorn, 1976).

Revelation: The Birth of a New Age, (Rainbow Bridge, 1978);
Vision of Findhorn Anthology, (Findhorn, 1976).

Sutphen, Dick, *You Were Born Again To Be Together,* (Pocket Books, 1976); *Past Lives, Future Loves,* (Pocket Books, 1978).

Tansley, David, *Omens of Awareness,* (N. Spearman, London, 1977).

Toben, Bob, *Space-Time and Beyond,* (Dutton, 1975).

Tompkins, Peter, and Christopher Bird, *The Secret Life of Plants,* (Harper & Row, 1973).

Weisman, Alan, *We, Immortals,* (Valley of the Sun, 1977).

Zukav, Gary, *The Dancing Wu Li Masters,* (Morrow Quill, 1979).

For further information, please write:

Mind Matters
P.O. Box 155
Washington Crossing, PA 18977